An Introduction to Integrative Psychotherapy

Also by the authors

PSYCHOTHERAPY SUPERVISION: An Integrative Relational Approach
to Psychotherapy Supervision (Open University Press, 2000)

An Introduction to Integrative Psychotherapy

Kenneth R. Evans

and

Maria C. Gilbert

First published in 2005 by
PALGRAVE MACMILLAN
Houndmills, Basingstoke, Hampshire RG21 6XS and
175 Fifth Avenue, New York, N.Y. 10010
Companies and representatives throughout the world.

PALGRAVE MACMILLAN is the global academic imprint of the Palgrave Macmillan division of St. Martin's Press, LLC and of Palgrave Macmillan Ltd. Macmillan® is a registered trademark in the United States, United Kingdom and other countries. Palgrave is a registered trademark in the European Union and other countries.

ISBN-13: 978–0–333–98726–1
ISBN-10: 0–333–98726–8

This book is printed on paper suitable for recycling and made from fully managed and sustained forest sources. Logging, pulping and manufacturing processes are expected to conform to the environmental regulations of the country of origin.

A catalogue record for this book is available from the British Library.

A catalog record for this book is available from the Library of Congress.

Printed in Great Britain by the
MPG Books Group, Bodmin and King's Lynn

We dedicate this book to the trainees who have challenged us, the colleagues who have supported us and to our children who continue to love us

Contents

Preface to an integrative relational model of
psychotherapy 1

Part 1 Philosophy, history and research **5**

1 Philosophy and values of integrative psychotherapy 7

2 The history of integration in psychotherapy 21

3 A basis in psychotherapy outcome studies
supports an integrative model 35

Part 2 Theoretical underpinnings **45**

4 A developmental–relational model for integration 47

5 The process of integrative psychotherapy and a
critique of the model 65

**Part 3 Clinical case study – the practical
application of theory** **81**

6 Assessment and diagnosis – 'It–It' relationship 83

7 Intrapsychic focus – 'I–It' relationship 101

8 Interpersonal focus – 'I–Thou' relationship 115

9 'I–Thou' mutuality – the end of the relationship 127

10 The parallel process in supervision 133

Part 4 Challenges and concerns **143**

11 Training integrative psychotherapists 145

12 Professional practice issues 157

Appendix 167

Bibliography 174

Index 183

Preface to an integrative relational model of psychotherapy

In the domain of integration the term 'integrative' has had many definitions and applications. Generally, the term refers to any orientation in psychotherapy that exemplifies, or is developing towards, a conceptually coherent, principled theoretical combination of two or more specific approaches, or represents a new meta-theoretical model of integration in its own right. In the literature, some distinction is usually made between 'integration' and 'eclecticism'; integration is often depicted as a comprehensive and internally coherent process, whereas eclecticism generally refers to a more random process of choosing 'what works' in a particular instance, without concern for the neatness of theoretical fit with the original pure-form approach or without a particular desire for theoretical coherence. However, given the dynamic manner in which most clinicians in practice embark on an integrative process, the latter could be seen as a stage along the way, as the person goes through a process of growth and change and gradually develops a new individual style of working. In the course of this development many of us went through a stage in which we may have said that we 'draw on several approaches depending on the client's needs'. With regard to this process of development, Norcross and Goldfried suggest that in the general field of integration: 'The primary distinction is between empirical pragmatism and theoretical flexibility. Integration refers to a commitment to a conceptual or theoretical creation beyond eclecticism's pragmatic blending of procedures' (Norcross and Goldfried, 1992, p. 12). The aim of this book is to provide the reader with a framework for integration, based in a relationship paradigm, with sufficient flexibility for a creative match with diverse client needs and contexts.

Chapter 1 of this book reviews the philosophical basis for integration. Chapter 2 reviews the history of integration and looks at different ways in which the process of integration has been conceptualized in the field, which is followed by a discussion in Chapter 3 of the basis in outcome research for an integrative approach to psychotherapy. In Chapter 4, we present our developmental-relational model for integration based on a view of different dimensions of the self and self-development, followed in Chapter 5 by a look at the process of psychotherapy from an intersubjective integrative perspective related to a view of the self-in-relationship. Chapters 6 through 9 cover the application of our model to therapeutic practice in the form of an extended case study followed in Chapter 10 with some reflections on the parallel process in supervision. Chapter 11 explores issues to do with the clinical training of integrative psychotherapists in which we somewhat boldly publish a list of suggested core competencies for the integrative psychotherapist. We conclude in Chapter 12 with a review of some professional concerns as these affect integrative psychotherapists in the field.

Our own approach to integration, while affirming the importance of foregrounding particular approaches or combinations of approaches to specific problems, nevertheless places the highest priority on those elements which are common to all psychotherapies, especially the centrality of the therapeutic relationship in all its dimensions. Such a relational approach to integration affirms the importance of providing a holding environment in which growth and healing can take place in an intersubjective space that has been co-created by both client and therapist. This emphasis on the co-construction of relationship means that we support a 'two-person' view of the therapeutic process in which both participants are constantly viewed as contributing to a shared relationship in a delicate dance of mutual interaction and influence.

We stress the importance of the client as an architect of change at the same time as we honour the quality of the therapist's presence in the relationship. The therapeutic process is seen as a joint endeavour and each therapeutic relationship as unique in its dyadic qualities. The therapeutic relationship always takes place in a particular social, political, historical and spiritual context which will influence the nature of the interaction between the people. We, therefore, place an ongoing emphasis on the wider context in which the therapeutic dyad is located in all its dimensions and complexity. This approach focuses on the immediacy of the therapeutic encounter as central to the therapeutic process and as the medium or container for change within an ever-changing field. In this process we honour the place for creativity in technique and strategies as these emerge from the relational context and organically facilitate the therapeutic process.

The theme which runs through our relational–developmental approach to integration is the concept of the 'developing self'. We speak rather of the self-in-relationship since self and environment are inextricably linked and are interdependent. We consider that the 'self' of the person continues to develop and evolve at increasing levels of complexity across the lifespan as the person responds to new relationships and new challenges at different developmental stages. Our central focus is on the self-in-relationship since we see the person as indelibly linked into her environment and never existing or developing separately from context. Along with writers like Kohut (1977) and subsequent self psychologists, we regard the self as the superordinate organizing principle in the personality which is at the heart of our experience of 'selfness' and uniqueness, as well as forming a bridge to the rest of humanity and the natural world around us. We all continually strive to achieve and maintain a sense of self-coherence which provides stability in our experience in relation to ourselves and others, and in relation to the animate and inanimate world around us.

In the process of developing the concept of the evolving self-in-relationship, we explore six different domains of self-relatedness:

1. *The biological domain*: the relationship of self to body. This refers to the relationship that I, myself, have with my own body. Here we explore a person's experience of self as a living, breathing entity; how the person animates his own body and the relationship he has with his bodily self.
2. *The intrapsychic domain*: the relationship of self to self. This refers to the internal world of experience of the person,

including the dialogues between different parts of the self and how these are constituted and develop over time. We look at ways of understanding the nature and functioning of a person's frame of reference which forms the basis of the experience of self-in-the-world.

3. *The interpersonal domain*: the relationship of self to others. Here we look at the realm of interpersonal relationships and how we negotiate our relatedness with others. We look at the importance of the attachment process and the inter-subjective, mutually interactive quality of early relationships that create the template for later relating and of self–object needs throughout the lifespan.

4. *The intercultural and contextual domain*: the relationship of self to context. Here we look at the embeddedness of self experience in our context. We consider the social, political, historical, economic, cultural and organizational influences on the ever-developing sense of self.

5. *The ecological domain*: the relationship of self to the physical environment and to nature. Here we look at man's relation-ship with the natural world and at how his sensitivity or lack of sensitivity to nature may influence his being-in-the-world.

6. *The transcendental domain*: the relationship of self to the transpersonal and spiritual world. Here we look at man's search for a meaning wider than his own existence and the manner in which this may be achieved by the developing spiritual self of the person.

Central to our discussion of the self-in-relationship in the ever-unfolding developmental process over the lifespan, is Buber's (1996) concept of the 'I–Thou' relationship. We consider that I–Thou relating is vital for the healthy development of a sense of self that is vibrant and cohesive. In such an I–Thou relational process the person values self and other in a respectful mutual interaction. Where this respectful mutuality is absent, a person is vulnerable to shame and to a fragmentation of the self. In this sense, a presentation of our model also involves a perspec-tive on derailments that occur in self–other relating and the consequences of these for the individual. We then look at how such derailments or deficits may be healed through the mutuality of an effective therapeutic relationship.

Part 1

Philosophy, history and research

1

Philosophy and values of integrative psychotherapy

Why a chapter on philosophy and values?

We believe that epistemology (theories of knowledge) is fundamentally important to an understanding of any approach to psychotherapy. Without at least a general knowledge of the philosophical bases of a psychotherapy model it is impossible to adequately critique the theory underpinning the model or the values conveyed in the clinical application of the model. It is absurd to assume that a psychotherapist can suspend her values, which may sometimes be explicit but always implicit in her behaviour and attitudes. Knowledge is instrumental to power and it is never politically innocent (Tanesini, 1999). So it is highly relevant to ask what power, apparent or implicit in its values, might a psychotherapy method, assuming any particular form of knowledge, convey to the client?

Fundamental to our approach to integrative psychotherapy will be the notion of the psychotherapist as a 'reflexive practitioner' based on the practice of 'critical subjectivity' (Reason, 1994). The reflective function as defined by Fonaghy *et al.* (2002) is 'the capacity to envision mental states in self and others' and enables us to conceptualize 'others' beliefs, feelings, attitudes, desires, hopes, knowledge, imagination, pretense, deceit, intentions, plans ...' as different from our own (p. 24). We therefore intend to set out clearly in this chapter the philosophies upon which our approach to integrative psychotherapy is based and the values we derive from them, as a necessary prerequisite to an understanding and appreciation of our approach together with an informed basis for constructive criticism. We trust that this will be experienced as an invitation to dialogue and creative innovation.

First we feel compelled to ask, are there really 480 different kinds of psychotherapy as reported by Karuso? (quoted in Dryden and Norcross, 1990, p. 184). Or could it be that a number of theorists from different models of psychotherapy share some central tenets but express them differently and in different therapeutic languages? Arguably the increasing movement towards psychotherapy integration would suggest greater commonality than is often realized or acknowledged but it is difficult to judge since therapists rarely appear to establish or question the epistemological assumptions underlying their theories, models and approaches thus making it difficult to compare and contrast (Mace, 1999). Goldfried's plea for a common language for case formulation seems to us an attempt to find existing commonalities in conceptualization and create the bridge between different orientations (Goldfried, 1995b).

There is some evidence to suggest that what attracts therapists to a particular school of therapy are personal reasons rather than 'neutral objectivity or logic' (Barton, 1974). Frank and Frank (1991) go as far as to suggest that it is belief that is central to an understanding and application of any psychotherapeutic approach. While therapeutic progress requires sufficient belief in the therapeutic method, on the part of both therapist and client, we agree with Downing that it is dangerous when those beliefs are held as absolute truths rather than as temporary and open to critique (Downing, 2000). There is also a sense that when people have invested large amounts of time and money in training in a particular approach, it may be difficult to critically challenge that allegiance.

Over the past 20 years or so we have witnessed an important trend towards a more ecumenical spirit among the psychotherapies represented in the United Kingdom Council for Psychotherapy (UKCP) and the European Association for Psychotherapy (EAP) and evidenced in the range of issues explored at professional conferences and published in The Psychotherapist, the journal of the UKCP, the International Journal of Psychotherapy EAP and the Journal of Psychotherapy Integration (SEPI). All three of these organisations require high levels of cooperation among and between the different approaches represented to maintain collaboration and dialogue. However, while acknowledging the significance of these developments it is abundantly clear that the 'many' schools of psychotherapy exist in relative isolation from each other with regard to access to and interest in 'rival' theories. Indeed the proliferation of 'different' schools of psychotherapy can be likened to the proliferation of religious denominations following the breakdown in the monopoly of the Roman Catholic Church. It appears to us that within each psychotherapy 'denomination' there is a fundamentalist element that preserves the founding teachings relatively unchanged and holds them to be universally valid for all time, thereby underpinning dogma rather than supporting dialogue and critique. No wonder those brave enough to disagree can feel their views are tantamount to heresy and may go underground. Perhaps this is a contributory factor in the proliferation of 'schools' since a controversial idea may ultimately be forced to find a new home elsewhere?

Sophie Freud in a public lecture criticized her grandfather Sigmund Freud, together with Carl Jung as 'false prophets' by encouraging dependency and uncritical adherence among their 'disciples' (Freud, 2002). Her plea that we should relate to the leaders in the psychotherapy profession as 'brothers and sisters' rather than 'fathers and mothers' supports our view of the psychotherapist as a reflexive practitioner rather than a disciple. The education and training of psychotherapists must bear some responsibility for this process. As Downing asserts,

> while some doubts are tolerated by a training programme, challenges to the core assumption of the approach are usually discouraged, dismissed or treated as 'resistance'. The trainee learns rather quickly that there are ways of experiencing, behaving, and verbalizing which receive praise and reward from the mentors, and those that are greeted with raised eyebrows, silence, or even rebuke. (Downing, 2000, p. 39).

In our trainings it becomes incumbent upon us to foster dialogue across differences and respect individuality of developing frameworks and thinking.

In order to fully appreciate contemporary philosophical influences on psychotherapy we believe it is important to first understand the historical context out of which current philosophical ideas have emerged. Kuhn (1962) introduced us to the idea of paradigms, which are a way of looking at ourselves and the world that give meaning to our lives and shape an entire cultural age. A paradigm shift requires new theories and new assumptions that are contrary to and incompatible with prevailing theory(s) and bring about major changes in what is considered worthy of consideration for inquiry and inclusion in the field of study.

It is possible to distinguish three such paradigms or world views within western philosophy, religion and science. The Classical or pre-Modern Age culminated in Greece (429–347 BC) with the Platonic notion that all reality was based on ideals and forms which transcended human reason. Truth was universal because it was grounded in universal forms such as beauty, goodness, justice etc. Such forms were metaphysical and human knowledge was contingent on the existence of these forms. Within the Jewish and Christian traditions this was manifest in the notion of God as creator and everything, including human beings, were contingent upon God. Sin destroys our relationship with God and to restore the relationship we need to respond to revelation, repent and have faith. Faith results in a new form of knowledge – revealed knowledge. Truth is universal because it is grounded in an eternal and external creator.

In the seventeenth and eighteenth centuries the Modern Age, or Age of Enlightenment, moved knowledge beyond superstition and religious dogma and instead put its trust in the power of reason. Observation, calculation, checking results, deducing conclusions, testing ideas, developing theories were all made possible by new inventions like the telescope and the prism. In the West people began to move out of the prison of dogma and fear of divine punishment. The experimental methods moved away from blind faith to observed fact. A process of de-centring the universe began. There was a paradigm shift from a theocentric to a ratiocentric way of thinking. The universe was rational and could be understood by reason. Truth was universal because human beings were rational. Descartes (1596–1650) epitomized this shift from dogma to reason with his famous statement 'I think therefore I am' as opposed to 'God is therefore I am.'

Now in the so-called postmodern Age we appear to have lost belief in emancipation and progress through knowledge and scientific research (Kvale, 1992). Personal knowledge and subjectivity are supported while objectivity is viewed with scepticism. According to Rosen 'knowledge and meaning are constructed and reconstructed over time and within the social matrix. They do not constitute universal and immutable essences or objective truths existing for all times and cultures' (Rosen, 1996, p. 20). The essential reality of nature is therefore not separate and complete such that it can no longer be examined objectively and from outside. From a postmodern perspective there is no single, universal, privileged, accurate, truthful and secure way of understanding anything, including people! We are sympathetic to Loewenthal who writes, 'Postmodernism blows the whistle on scientific intellectualism as one more form of Victorian morality which inappropriately tries to establish itself in relation to people' (Loewenthal, 1996).

The general tone of postmodernism is curious, confused, pluralist, fragmentary and open-ended and Tanesini (1999) believes that the idea of the postmodern expresses a widespread loss of faith in big ideals and theories. Lyotard (1996) describes the postmodern as 'incredulity toward metanarratives'. In the postmodern age 'It is no longer possible for psychotherapy to "intentionally or unintentionally" don the mantle of science through the seemingly scientific nature of their theoretical language, their therapeutic methods, or the locale of their practice' (Downing, 2000, p. 237). Indeed according to Heath 'psychotherapeutic theories are not theories: they are mind–mind myths and therefore cannot be empirically tested' (Heath, 2000).

The origins of psychoanalysis, and thus of psychotherapy, are located within the modernist frame of nineteenth-century liberal humanism when it was believed its hypotheses could be corroborated (Tolman, 1994). While liberal humanism has been criticized by Schopenhaur, Kierkegaard, Marx and Nietzche, and more recently feminist writers have been critical of Freud's ideas for being culturally encapsulated in Judaic-Christianity, paternalistic assumptions steeped in an eurocentric perspectives are supportive of the 'invidious relationship between the sexes, ratifying traditional roles and validating temperamental differences' (Millet, 1969, p. 78). A further criticism (in a similar vein) of psychotherapy across the broad spectrum of approaches is the emphasis on individual experience to the exclusion of contextual/social factors which tends to isolate the individual from his environment, context and external influences that may contribute to the root of their distress (Smail, 1998).

Alternatively the postmodern constructivist paradigm is based on 'a relativist ontology (multiple realities) a subjectivist epistemology (knower and respondent co-create meaning) and a naturalistic (in the natural world) set of methodologies' (Denzin and Lincoln, 2000). What this means in our everyday experience of living is summed up by Cushman, 'life is just a bridge, and a narrow one at that. It is shaky, and when there is a storm it swings back and forth too much. In times of trouble we will want for the bridge to be more than a bridge; we will try to pretend that it is solid aground. We might even, to assuage our fears, try to build a permanent house on it ... no theory can be a permanent house' (Cushman, 1995, p. 330).

Postmodernism challenges the foundations of what we know and how we know what we think we know through 'demystifying the great narrative of modernism' (Gergen, 1992, p. 28). It encourages inquiry and questioning of all phenomena and is thus supportive of the notion of the reflexive practitioner engaged in an ongoing process of enquiry and self-questioning.

We agree with Orange (1995, p. 46) that 'today most psychologists and philosophers agree that all experience ... is structured ... observation is theory-laden and presuppositionless knowing is impossible'. However, while '... the post-modern emphasis on stories or narratives is intended as a statement of modesty, there can be an easy slippage into reification of narrative as a foundational form of knowledge. This can in turn lead to implicit assumptions about "better" and more "appropriate" narratives for clients and to a notion of therapy as a form of story assessment and repair. In such a case, the appeal of post-modern plurality has been diverted back into modern singularity' (Lowe, 1999, p. 82). The assumption on the part of the therapist that his/her judgement is superior and will in the end govern the 'storyline' may become a form of oppression.

While absolute truth is neither as absolute nor as true as we may like to believe, the opposite polarity that truth is indistinguishable from opinion means that 'nothing is real, nothing is true and nothing is important' (Holland, 2000, p. 3). According to Holland modern scepticism as expressed, for example, in the writings of Jacques Derrida does not attempt to cultivate a new philosophy of life but rather to critique the theories and prejudices of others. But if we take everything apart then on what authority do we judge anything? 'Post-modern philosophy at its worst, presumes no authority at all except to claim with authority that there are no authorities' (Holland, 2000, p. 365). We have considerable sympathy with Holland when he concludes that 'neither the simplicity of grand narratives nor scepticism deal with the complexities, inconsistencies and paradoxes of real life' (Holland, 2000, p. 360). Perhaps in the end what is important is the ability to hold the tension between these polarities and accept that our own narratives may be culturally embedded, but at the same time not move to a position where there are no serious values or personal belief systems allowed for fear of becoming petrified in stone!

Lawson asks, 'since we cannot stay where we are, and since a return to some form of realism is not a possible strategy, we must look elsewhere if we are to find a means to escape the contemporary predicament. But where might we look, and how?' (Lawson, 2001, p. xxxvii).

We believe that what is needed is a position between the nihilism of deconstructionism and the naivety of structuralism. Some have sought to establish this 'middle ground' based on pragmatism. Black and Holford, for example, maintain that from a postmodern perspective it is not important as to whether something is right or wrong, true or false but whether it works (Black and Holford, 1999). In similar vein Polkinghorne writes, 'one does not ask if a knowledge claim is an accurate depiction of the real – is it true? One asks, rather, does acting on this knowledge claim produce successful results' (Polkinghorne, 1992, p. 151).

Others like Holland believe that liberal democracy has become complacent, failed to understand and nurture spiritual needs and sold out to commerce at the expense of human values. Nevertheless it may be possible to breathe new life into current structures rather than destroy it without a viable replacement. We agree and set out below to establish a 'middle ground' between conviction and uncertainty where, with Downing, we attempt to avoid our assumptions becoming reified in dogma and at the same time avoid the ultimate impotence of unyielding scepticism (Downing, 2000). We agree with Bernstein that there is an intrinsic relationship between absolutism and nihilism in that either polarity in the extreme obscures the other and is liable to become dogmatic (Bernstein, 1992). We suggest, therefore, that a way through this demise is to consider polarities from a paradoxical rather than an oppositional perspective.

Perls and his co-workers (Perls *et al.*, 1951/94) believed that polarities were dialectical forming two ends of one continuum (Clarkson and Mackewn, 1993). You cannot have one without the other, for example, good – bad, right – wrong, structuralism – deconstructivism, absolutism – nihilism; the one defines the other. The so-called opposite characteristics do not contradict each other but instead form two sides of the same coin. In Perls' paradoxical view, when one characteristic is foreground another polarity remains present in the background and it is possible to work with both polarities bringing both characteristics into awareness. In this way one can affirm the validity of both ends of the polarization. Polarization entails 'either – or' categories which can become stuck and impervious to change (Kelly, 1955), and into which one classifies events or perceptions (Korb *et al.*, 1989). The polarization of attitudes, feelings and behaviours tend to rigidify a person's view of self, others and the world. Polarization is appealing because it appears to offer certainty and thus security in an uncertain world – '... polarising of feelings, attitudes and values enable the individual to establish defining bases for relating to the world' (Korb *et al.*, 1989, p. 14). Polarization is arguably a prerequisite for fundamentalism for it can mean individuals strongly identifying with one polarity and denying the other. A dialectical approach to polarities helps to mitigate against seeing the truth as simple rather than complex.

This 'middle way' is a dialectical perspective and attitude to 'truth' which affirms the paradoxical nature of reality and, as such, is open to exploring the entire continuum between and including polarities. This requires a capacity for openness, a willingness for vulnerability, and the courage to sit with ambiguity and uncertainty (Gilbert and Evans, 2000). It involves a radical extension of Buber's I–Thou to facts, opinions, beliefs, evidence, and the like, as well as to people (Buber, 1923/96). It is this radical extension of dialogue that we maintain which exemplifies the postmodern spirit of open enquiry, rather than the nihilism of a scepticism that in extremis takes anti-rationalism to absurdity (Holland, 2000). 'You are therefore I am' may well underpin this philosophy!

Outlined below the epistemological bases of our approach to integrative psychotherapy. We do so with conviction and an openness to criticism that accepts them as being 'true for now'. With this attitude we hope to avoid the oppressive practice that can accompany belief in metanarratives and at the same time avoid the impotence to action that can accompany the more extreme expressions of constructivism and an absence of a belief in the importance of personal values.

The epistemological bases of our approach to integrative psychotherapy are interrelated and mutually supporting. Together they underpin the theory and method of our approach as well as providing the foundation for the values of our approach. In our opinion the epistemology, theory and clinical practice of any approach to psychotherapy should be consistent and explicit and thus accessible to critique.

Phenomenology

From the phenomenological perspective human behaviour is seen as determined by personal experience rather than by an external objective reality (Cohen and Manion, 1994). Emphasis is put upon direct experience and engagement, '... the most significant understandings that I have come to, I have not achieved from books or others, but initially, at least, from my direct perceptions, observations, and intuitions' (Moustakis, 1994, p. 41). The phenomenolgical method of enquiry honours the importance of subjective experience as a valid source of knowledge. Phenomenology is compatible with field theory.

Field theory

Field theory according to Lewin (1952) is a way of looking at the 'total situation', which has been described as the organised, interconnected, interdependent, interactive nature of human phenomena (Parlett, 1991). In this context what the field produces is viewed as having intrinsic meaning and value in itself. An experience is intimately connected with the current field conditions and cannot be understood in isolation. This underpins the importance of a sensitivity to the context of the client's life. Awareness is fundamental to field theory allowing the individual to become aware of, and to select from options available. Awareness requires that an individual has sufficient capacity for vulnerability and openness to experience, to promote nourishing contact with the environment. The gestalt notion of figure and ground is helpful in discerning on what of the totality of experience to focus attention on. At any point in our experience certain needs will take priority and become figural whilst others will remain in the ground of our experience. Attending to what is figural helps avoid being overwhelmed by all that is possible in the ground in the present. In focusing on the totality of experience at any given moment, field theory is compatible with holism.

Holism

Holism maintains that the whole is greater than the sum of the parts. From the holistic perspective nothing is deliberately ignored. Observation of the happenings in the external world is made parallely with observations of one's inner subjective world. Holistic observation is therefore not simply 'looking' but rather looking mindfully and in depth. The holistic process offers active involved observation in all of one's being including cognition, sensation and emotion. One attempts to bring the whole of oneself to what is figural in the whole of one's engagement with the world. This may be viewed as the interface between the 'dialectical-intrapsychic' level of experience and the 'dialogical-interpersonal' (Hycner, 1995, p. 74) in the context of a person's total experience.

Dialogue

Thus the epistemological bases of our approach to integrative psychotherapy supports the non-linear and multicausality of field theory, the illumination of subjective personal experience of phenomenology, and the simultaneous exploration of both inner experience and outer engagement with the environment of holism.

The dialogical perspective developed by the existential philosopher Martin Buber is compatible with all the above epistemologies and adds a further dimension crucial to our approach to integrative psychotherapy – the interhuman dimension. Buber criticized the overemphasis on individual existence at the expense of human inter-existence. The inter-human focus of Buber incorporates both the I–Thou and I–It polarities of living and confirms our conviction that a paradoxical perspective towards polarities best fits the human condition. I–It is necessary for living, said Buber, and at the same time, without the I–Thou we do not really live! (Buber, 1996).

The co-creation of dialogue and an adherence to a two-person view of psychotherapy

Buber's emphasis on the I–Thou of relationship leads naturally to a belief in the co-creation or co-construction of all relationships. Central to our conception of psychotherapy is a focus on the co-creation of the therapeutic relationship as an interactional event in which both parties participate. It is not a one-sided relationship in which one party 'does' to the other while the other is a passive recipient, but rather a constantly evolving co-constructed relational process to which client and therapist alike contribute. This is very much a two-person view of the therapeutic process, acknowledging that the client too will impact on the therapist in an ongoing way. Our approach is very much in line with intersubjectivity theory which emphasizes 'reciprocal mutual influence' (Stolorow and Atwood, 1992, p. 18), contemporary dialogic approaches within gestalt with the focus on the healing dialogue in psychotherapy (Hycner, 1993) and contemporary relational psychoanalysis with this tenet: 'The relational approach that I am advancing views the patient–analyst relationship as continually established and reestablished through ongoing mutual influence in which both patient and analyst systematically affect, and are affected by, each other' (Aron, 1999, p. 248). Stolorow and Atwood (1992) succinctly summarize their position: '... our view [is] that ... the trajectory of self experience is shaped at every point in development by the intersubjective system in which it crystalizes' (p. 18). They use the term 'codetermination' to describe this reciprocal process in development and in psychotherapy (op. cit., p. 24). These three approaches all stress the mutuality of the therapeutic process, although the techniques used, views of transference and counter-transference, and the manner of relating varies widely.

Values

The following statement of values follow from the above philosophies and we have specifically constructed them for application to clinical practice.

1. The client's subjective experience is his truth and the starting point of exploration. In integrative psychotherapy accepting what is given and honouring the client's world as it is for them is the therapist's primary responsibility.
2. The 'now' is the present awareness of the client and the only moment in which they have any direct control. The 'now' may be overwhelmed by the past, as with transference, or by future anxiety as in anxiety states but such experience is in the 'now'. The client discovers in the now what is moral in accordance with their own choices and values.
3. People are response-able, the primary agents in determining their own behaviour. However, we see people as embedded in their context which may limit the options open to them, sometimes in crippling ways.
4. Morality at its best is based on organismic needs – on a relatively accurate knowledge of what is, rather than 'shouldistic' – based on an arbitrary imposition of what others think. This applies to the regulation of interpersonal

relationships, to intrapsychic regulation and to regulation within social groups.

5. Given that the client has a choice of behaviour in the 'now' the therapist works on increasing the client's awareness of antecedence, organismic reaction and consequences of behaviour. Thus the therapist 'explores' rather than 'modifies' behaviours.

6. The therapeutic relationship is a microcosm of the client's 'way of being-in-the-world' and so the client may see and hear how they are experienced by the therapist. Therefore, it is important that the therapist's active presence is authentic and energised, honest and direct. This demands the therapist [be] cognisant of the counter-transference and has developed significant self-awareness to monitor the process and in particular the potential for the abuse of power in the therapeutic relationship.

7. In organismic self-regulation choosing and learning happen with a natural integration of mind and body, thought and feeling, physical and spiritual, self and environment, that is, holistically.

8. Change is possible and occurs holistically when a person becomes who and what they are and not when they try to become what they are not. Paradoxically change takes place not through coercion but if a person takes the time and effort to become themselves (Beisser, A. R., 1970).

9. Life is in constant flux. Therapy not only affects the world but the world impacts the therapy. Personal growth and development are possible and requires intrapsychic, interpersonal and socio-political awareness to deconstruct and reconstruct knowledge, awareness and understanding.

10. Environmental factors prove a major source of distress, disempowerment and alienation. This is particularly manifest in inequality of opportunity and oppressive practice. Integrative psychotherapy upholds a person's right to be different and this requires challenging and confronting racism, sexism, ageism and class.

11. Dialogue is a manifestation of the existential perspective on relationship. Buber's notion of 'meaning' through meeting supports the view of therapy as a 'co creation' – the notion that 'truth' begins with two. The personal 'I'

has meaning only in relation to an other, in the I–Thou dialogue or in I–It contact. Dialogue is based on experiencing the other person as they are and experiencing oneself – sharing the reciprocity and cooperation which in turn requires a willingness to be responsible and authentic. Dialogue is supported by modern feminist thought maintaining the importance of relationship and affiliation in the development of identity and dialogue, reciprocity and cooperation in the pursuit of understanding.

12. Maturity is therefore not simply about autonomy of self but self-in-relation and is a continuous process of creative adjustment throughout life. Indeed health may be described as the creative interplay between the individual and the environment. Adjustment without creativity is conformity to an external standard and conflicts with phenomenology. Creativity without adjustment is nihilism and conflicts with dialogue.

13. Both self in isolation and self in negative manipulation of the environment can be oppressive – a form of violence to self or other. Violence is viewed as an attempt at annihilation of self or other that is antithetical to awareness and the open expression of I–Thou.

14. Self and other(s) may be viewed with curiosity and compassion rather than negative judgement.

15. Integrative psychotherapy seeks to promote sufficient integration that maximizes that which continues to develop after the therapy session and in the 'absence' of the therapist. This supports the client's right to self-determination and personal dignity.

2 The history of integration in psychotherapy

The development of three main streams of thought in psychology, first in relative isolation and in opposition to one another, and then the gradual building of bridges across these traditions, marks the history of the integrative movement. All the traditions have contributed invaluable insights into the working of the human mind. Psychoanalysis has given us an understanding of unconscious processes and how these may affect all our experience. With its focus on the importance of transference, psychoanalysis has also emphasized how relationships from the past may be recreated in the present out of conscious awareness and have far-reaching effects on our lives. Behaviourism has given us an understanding of how sensitive we are in the learning process to positive and negative reinforcement: that behaviour that is reinforced, even if negatively, will tend to persist. However, what can be learnt can also be unlearnt and replaced with more adaptive behaviours. Humanistic psychology has added a belief in the person's potential and capacity for self-healing in our drive for self-actualization. Clarkson (1992) in her map of the three major traditions in psychology, points out that psychoanalysis focuses on the question, 'Why?' and looks for understanding and insight. Behaviourism focuses on the question, 'What?' and looks to what behaviours are dysfunctional and in need of change. Whereas humanism asks the question, 'How?', that is, how does the person feel and how does the person experience sensations, emotions and the sensory world of experience? (Clarkson, 1992, p. 3). To this we may add systems-theory that looks at the embeddedness of the person in his context and asks the question, 'Where?', where is the problem located in time and place, assuming that the problem is always a systems-issue; and existentialism that focuses on issues of

21

meaning, death and isolation that all human beings share and perhaps could best be said to focus on the question, 'Wherefore?' or wherein lies the meaning of man's existence.

The search for integration has resulted in part from the perceived shortcomings in the three main schools or traditions of psychotherapy. Psychoanalysis has been criticized for the excessive length of the treatment and its lack of focus on specific behavioural changes. It has been pointed out that people may gather many insights into themselves in the process of analysis but still repeat old destructive patterns of behaviour. Behaviour therapy, whilst focusing on specific desired behavioural changes has been accused of achieving symptom resolution whilst not dealing with the deeper underlying structural problems. This may often result in what has been termed 'symptom substitution' as the person substitutes one symptom for another, leaving the underlying problem untouched. Humanistic therapies with their emphasis on growth potential, optimal functioning and self-actualization have been accused of being over-optimistic and minimizing the shadow side of experience and downplaying the existential realities of the human condition. Integration evolved in part, in response to these perceived shortcomings in particular approaches and from the needs of clinicians in the field to find more effective ways of helping their clients.

The initial lack of dialogue across approaches and the ostensibly incompatible views taken about human experience is well illustrated by the experience of one of the authors whose first study of psychology was in the late 1950s. The first year of her psychology course was divided into two semesters: the first on behaviourism and the second on psychoanalysis. What has remained vividly in her memory are these statements from the behaviourist semester: 'Only attend to observable behaviour; what you can see and measure is relevant to experience, nothing else is' and 'There is no personality, only behaviour.' From the psychoanalytic semester, 'Nothing is what it seems on the surface; you can only get at the truth of behaviour indirectly through dreams, slips of the tongue and other indirect messages from the unconscious'; 'Surface behaviour is a disguise for repressed material that lies deep in the unconscious; do not focus on overt behaviour or you will only achieve symptom relief not deep structural change.' These presentations did highlight the basically different visions of these approaches, what Messer referred to as the 'comic vision' in behaviourism and the 'ironic and tragic vision' of psychoanalysis (Messer, 2001). The two approaches did seem to agree that there was no such concept as personality and neither spoke much, if at all, about social interaction! There was no attempt at a debate in the course, nor even a comment about these widely differing views. Fortunately since then, the history of the integrative movement has made many rapprochements across these at one time unbridgeable divides and opened up a rich and varied dialogue!

We are indebted to Goldfried's (1995a) interesting and comprehensive account of the history of integration over the past 70 years from which we have selected a few highlights for our short account that follows. As Goldfried (1995a) points out, the rapprochement between behaviourism and psychoanalysis has a long history starting as early as 1932 when French raised the challenging question at the 88th meeting of the American Psychiatric Association of whether the psychoanalytic concept of repression was perhaps similar to the behavioural concept of extinction. In a fascinating paper, French outlines similarities in their respective presentation of the traumatic effects on the learning process that purportedly links the work of Pavlov with that of Freud. French points out that in Pavlov's work a conditioned reflex that has been experimentally extinguished is not permanently destroyed, 'just as in our psychoanalytic experience we find that there are varying depths of repression' (French, 1933, p. 1169). French's paper marked a historical moment in raising the idea that we were perhaps looking at similar processes from different perspectives, an approach to integration that has continued in the attempt to find a common language for psychotherapy to facilitate dialogue across orientations (Goldfried, 1995b).

In 1936, Rozenweig made a contribution of a related though somewhat different kind in looking at three common factors across orientations in psychotherapy. He maintained that regardless of orientation it is the personality of the therapist that influences the effectiveness of the process; that interpretations offer clients an alternative way of looking at things; and that change in one area will have a spin-off effect in another, so different orientations may focus on different areas but still get positive outcomes (outlined in Goldfried, 1995b). This interesting focus on common factors across orientations as a basis for integration runs as an important thread through the history of the integrative movement.

Dollard and Miller's (1950) classic book 'Personality and Psychotherapy' marks another milestone in the integrative movement. Again this was an attempt to build a bridge between psychoanalysis and behaviourism. Dollard and Miller describes in detail how psychoanalytic concepts such as regression, anxiety, repression and displacement might be understood within the framework of learning theory (Goldfried, 1995b). They were interested in the integration of different theoretical concepts across orientations, a forerunner we believe to later endeavours to find a common language for the psychotherapies. Goldfried (1995b) points out that Dollard and Miller's book was continually in print for over 30 years; it is hard not to see this as some enduring testament to their efforts at integration! In essence, their integration may be viewed as an attempt at reconciling complementary ways of viewing psychological processes and building bridges between psychoanalysis and behaviourism.

These early efforts were followed in the 1960s and 1970s by further efforts to look at commonalities across therapies as Frank (1982) did when he listed the common 'healing factors' in therapy such as the client's expectancy and hope of being helped and the tendency of psychotherapy to correct misconceptions that people held of themselves and others. Gradually, more adherents of humanism, behaviourism and psychoanalysis became open to approaches to client work and concepts from the other traditions, as exemplified by Wachtel's (1977) view that psychoanalysis and behaviour therapy could mutually complement one another in the interests of the client.

The integrative movement has gradually gathered strength to the effect that even Roth and Fonaghy (1996) in their critical review of psychotherapy outcome research that advocates particular treatments for particular problems, make the following statement in favour of integration: 'Ultimately, theoretical orientations will have to be integrated since they are all approximate models of the same phenomenon: the mind in distress' (p. 12). At present they maintain that integration may create confusion rather than clarify controversies so they do not currently advocate this route. However, we as proponents of integration, ally ourselves with the many integrationists who are steadily developing and expanding different models of integration in their endeavour to be flexible and to give the best possible service to the client, based on clinical experience and outcome research in the field of psychotherapy.

We shall now review some ways in which different approaches to integration have been conceptualized over time to give the reader a sense of the wealth of the field. The questions that are always in the background for us in viewing the integrative movement can be summed up as follows:

1. Are there actually as many models of therapy as there are people practising as therapists?
2. Are we searching for the impossible dream in looking for common models of integration that could unite therapists from differing origins?
3. Have we ignored the client as the architect of change and focused too exclusively on what the therapist provides?
4. Is developing an overarching meta-theoretical integrative model an impossibly ambitious project?

Stricker and Gold (1996) write of three different approaches to integration: theoretical integration; technical eclecticism; and the common factors approach. We shall discuss each of these in turn and then move on to other ways in which integration has been conceptualized.

Theoretical integration: the ideal optimistic but utopian view

This refers to the creation of a meta-model of therapy or a therapy of therapies. The attempt to create such meta-theoretical models of integration has been labelled impossible by some and grandiose by others because these critics view as formidable any attempt at a rapprochement on this meta-theoretical level. However, several meta-theoretical models have been developed and have proved an excellent support for clinicians in practice by providing them with an overall map or narrative on which to base their integrative practice. Mahrer (1989) when writing about different approaches to integration, states that 'for those who are concerned with integrating psychotherapies, the most promising gateway is a significantly modified theory of human beings' (p. 68).

This may seem a too ambitious project to some, yet we believe that as practising clinicians many of us are constantly updating our theory of human beings as we come into contact with new information, for example, from developmental psychology or neurobiology. This process often happens outside of our conscious awareness. Our implicit theories may differ vastly from what we say and believe we do, which could provide an interesting area for reflection and research.

Several people have made an attempt to develop such meta-theoretical models of integration: inter alia, Wilber (1980) who in his model tracks the process of psychospiritual development that people move through in the life cycle; Clarkson's (1990) five-relationship model, which bridges the three major traditions of psychotherapy in its emphasis on the centrality of the therapeutic relationship; Clarkson has also along with Lapworth (1992) presented a seven-level model for understanding human functioning and informing clinical choices; Opazo (1997) has provided a supraparadigmatic model which spans the individual, social and ecological systems in which the individual exists. These models have in common the attempt to create a theory of theories: a meta-model that spans all approaches to psychotherapy in an effort to facilitate integration and make sense of a multiplicity of seeming contradictions between theories. Often such meta-models focus on the commonalities between therapies as a basis for their integration.

Technical eclecticism: the pragmatic and adaptive but incomplete view

The phrase 'what works for what problem' may be said to pick up on the spirit of much eclecticism in psychotherapy which focuses on the immediate pragmatic choice of intervention. Eclecticism refers to empirically based forms of integration that focus on what works with a particular client for a particular problem. Eclectic approaches vary from the haphazard and the arbitrary to the idiosyncratic to the systematic, empirically validated models of treatment selection. Such eclectic approaches are not related to any particular theory of personality or psychopathology but are based more on empirical research recommendations. Lazarus (1981) who describes himself as a 'technical eclectic' has developed his multi-modal approach to therapy on the basis of a careful assessment of the client's problem, followed by the choice of relevant techniques from different orientations in a systematic manner in order to assist the client most effectively. He claims to make no attempt at a meta-theory of integration nor does he express any interest in such an endeavour.

Critics of eclecticism have pointed out that there is sometimes no account taken of the incompatibility of an 'imported' technique with other aspects of the therapist's practice and this could lead to detrimental outcomes for the client. For example, if 'two-chair work' is used ad hoc this could induce pathological regression in a client with a fragile sense of self without an awareness on the part of the therapist of the risks involved in such a technique out of the context of its 'parent' theory. However, in practice many clinicians do import techniques and strategies after careful thought and with clear benefit to their clients. The systematic approach advocated by Lazarus (1981) is an attempt to avoid a haphazard approach to intervention.

Common factors: a logical compromise but perhaps a restricted view?

The search for common factors across psychotherapies dates from the 1930s; in the intervening period, both outcome research and clinical experience have contributed to the debate. To some extent this process may have been hampered because many people feel a loyalty to their own 'pure-form' approach and are not particularly committed to showing that the method that they have spent time, effort and often great expense in acquiring, can be equated with any other in terms of concepts or outcomes.

In a review of the literature, Goldfried and Padawer (1982 quoted by Goldfried, 1995b, p. 203) list the following areas of commonality amongst approaches:

1. The culturally induced expectation that therapy can be helpful so that most interventions feed into the person's expectation that therapy is generally a helpful thing to undergo. This is spoken of by Yalom (1985) as 'the instillation of hope'.
2. The participation in a psychotherapeutic relationship, that is, the provision of an accepting, caring and attentive relationship is of itself beneficial to people. This was stressed by Rogers (1951) as the basic ingredient of effective therapy and is often a unique experience in the person's life.
3. The possibility of obtaining an external perspective on oneself and the world: through the feedback provided by therapy, a person attains a change in frame of reference and is able to change self perception.
4. The encouragement of corrective emotional experiences: there seems to be agreement that new experiences form a crucial component of therapy, whether these take place primarily within the session or between sessions.
5. The opportunity to repeatedly test reality: this involves a combination of gaining a new perspective on the self from external feedback and the practising and consolidating of new behaviours and responses in a supportive atmosphere.

A criticism of the common-factors approach to therapy maintains that if integration were based on common factors alone we might lose the richness of many highly developed theories and techniques. Yet, there is really no reason why we cannot honour common factors in the healing process, and at the same time use those techniques and strategies that are compatible with our own and the client's frame of reference. We believe that all therapists inevitably develop their own individual style of working as they become more experienced. In effect as the Fiedler study of the 1950s first suggested, there is a growing similarity between experienced practitioners from different orientations as they become immersed in their clinical practice. Fiedler, showed that there are often greater similarities between experienced clinicians from different orientations than between beginners and advanced clinicians of the same orientation (Fiedler, 1950). It seems that the process of integration may occur naturally as people respond to their clients' needs.

Goldfried (1995b) has also committed himself to the task of finding a common language for psychotherapy that spans different approaches. He believes that such a language would enable people of different theoretical orientations to hold a clinical dialogue using concepts about which there is agreement across approaches. One such example, used by Goldfried in his article on finding a common language for case formulation, is the use of the term 'vicious and virtuous cycles' to describe, repetitive destructive patterns in people's lives and the constructive alternatives to these which form much of the focus of our everyday therapeutic endeavours (Goldfried, 1995b). The term 'vicious cycle' can find its equivalent in psychoanalysis as 'the neurotic repetition compulsion', in transactional analysis as 'the game', in gestalt psychotherapy as 'the fixed gestalt', and in cognitive therapy as 'the core schema', inter alia. However, clinicians often tend to be wedded to their own particular therapeutic language which can prevent them from realizing that someone else is referring to a similar manifestation. A common everyday language could serve to bridge this gap and help us to establish where we agree and where indeed we do disagree! For example, Erskine and Trautmann's (1996) excellent translation of the concepts of self psychology into reader-friendly everyday language marks another such endeavour at finding common terminology for complex concepts.

Assimilative integration: a therapeutic advance or simply an attenuation of the original 'pure-form approach'?

In 1992 Messer introduced the concept of assimilative integration as the most likely and possible way forward in the field of integration. This refers to the gradual assimilation of techniques and concepts from other approaches into the therapist's original orientation. Assimilation proposes that when techniques from different theoretical approaches are incorporated into one's main theoretical orientation, their meaning interacts with the meaning of the 'host' theory. Both the imported technique and the pre-existing theory are mutually transformed and shaped into the final product. Hopefully for the better! The aim of assimilative integration is to retain the original theory whilst also incorporating those empirically supported interventions that will remediate the weaknesses of the therapist's existing approach and also those theoretical aspects that are compatible with, but are missing, from the current approach, trying to keep the result theoretically meaningful and clinically relevant.

Proponents of assimilative integration argue that this is the process that most practitioners go through as they become more experienced in response to the needs of their clients. The authors can see that we probably all, even out of awareness, import interventions and aspects of theory that we find clinically useful in the course of our practice. The risk involved here is that we might lose some of the power of the original approach if it becomes too diluted. Careful thought needs to be given to ensure the internal consistency of the emerging model: 'Unless the assimilative integrationist takes seriously the task of theory modification that is implied by the successful implementation of alternative techniques, these models will remain an inconsistent hybrid of theoretical purism and eclectic practice' (Wolfe, 2001).

Complementarity: combining the strengths of two approaches or diluting both?

Goldfried (1995a) suggested that much of integration could be understood in terms of commonality or complementarity. As commonality has been discussed at some length earlier, we shall look at complementarity here. Based on the premise that different approaches to psychotherapy may make differing unique contributions, adherents of complementarity hold that two or more distinct approaches could be usefully combined to maximize the effectiveness for the client. The strengths of both approaches then contribute to the final product. Cognitive-behaviour therapy is one such example, which has grown out of the awareness that a focus on changing manifest behaviour can be enhanced by taking into account the ways in which a person thinks and feels about himself in relation to this behaviour. Changes in the inner belief system are combined with a focus on changing manifest behaviour. Behaviour therapy was originally based on the concept of S-R (Stimulus is followed by Response) with no reference to the person as an intervening variable that could be directly worked with. Later this was changed to S-O-R (Stimulus-Organism-Response) when it was realized that working directly with a person's irrational thoughts and cognitions could substantially affect the process of change. Here tribute was being paid too to the powerful impact of a person's imaginative capacity on the way he shapes his behaviour, for better or for worse.

In Linehan's dialectical behaviour therapy (1993) combines principles of Zen acceptance and awareness with a Behaviour Therapy focus on overt behavioural change. This approach stresses paradoxically the importance of holding both the Zen polarity of acceptance of what is, and the focus on desired changes posited by behaviourism. Anthony Ryle's (1990) Cognitive-Analytic Therapy is another example of complementarity which combines psychodynamic concepts for exploring a person's internal process with Kelly's personal construct theory concerning our cognitive constructs, to provide an approach that is well suited to brief therapy and a focus on agreed outcomes and problem-solving manoeuvres.

We mention but a few of the rich complementary combinations that have emerged over the years as part of the integrative endeavour. These models have arisen as clinicians and researchers have looked beyond their own pure-form approaches to what may be gained by combining contrasting approaches and methods to the benefit of the client. The demands of a particular context or a particular group of clients and the desire of clinicians to help their clients with whatever is available have contributed to this developing process.

Neuroscience as a source for integration across therapies: a search for the impossible dream or a sound basis in science?

The recent resurgence of interest in neuroscience and neurobiology is offering another bridge to integration between clinicians from different orientations. The focus on the neuro-biological underpinnings of processes such as the attunement between the baby and the (m)other provide powerful evidence of the biological basis for attachment. The process of interaction between baby and (m)other leads to the building of neural connections that form the basis of the person's subsequent attachment pattern, his capacity for effective affect regulation and meta-cognitive processing all of which support effective functioning. Much of this communication happens at a non-verbal level which is highly affect-laden and forms part of a delicate and sensitive alignment and re-alignment process between parent and child that is internalized by the child as the process of affect regulation (Siegel, 1999).

From a therapeutic point of view, one of the most notable facts that has emerged from recent infant research is the inter-active and mutually regulatory nature of the parent–infant dyad which is mirrored in the therapeutic dyad. This idea of the co-creation of relationship underlies many of the contem-porary relational approaches to psychotherapy (Mitchell and Aron, 1999). Schore (1994) draws on research that suggests that right-hemisphere to right-hemisphere communication provided by the therapist in 'a right hemisphere dominant state of evenly hovering attention' (Schore, 2003) may well be a central healing factor in effective psychotherapy. This con-veying of empathy on a non-verbal level allows for the dys-regualtions in the patient to be gradually corrected in an atmosphere of mutuality. This research supports a view of psy-chotherapy as essentially relational where the quality of the therapeutic relationship is the primary healing process. We can see that these findings may well provide the bridge between approaches as different in their historical origins as relational psychoanalysis, gestalt dialogic therapy, self psychology, trans-actional analysis and the existential therapies. In many ways, this research is in its infancy and does not yet provide definitive evidence for the integrative endeavour. However, in our view, it has brought closer together into a more creative dialogue practitioners from diverse orientations and belief structures and bridged some long-standing barriers to communication across schools of therapy.

In conclusion

The information fuelling different approaches to integration has come from several sources: from theoreticians comparing different underlying assumptions; from clinicians in the field who gradually move towards a more integrative practice and from research into outcomes in psychotherapy. The comparison of the philosophical basis of different schools of psychotherapy has contributed information about a range of philosophical assumptions underlying practice, some of which are incompatible with one another, but is has also highlighted common assumptions between different approaches, for example, a shared focus by many on an holistic view of the person.

Clinicians in the field are often the first to experiment with new techniques and approaches as they face the challenge of helping clients effectively. New approaches to psychotherapy have evolved from this process. Kohut's development of self psychology grew out of the realization that traditional psychoanalysis did not seem appropriate to people with a narcissistic personality structure, who responded better to an approach rooted in empathy (Kohut, 1977). Current research into the neurobiological basis of child development is providing us with a model of the therapeutic dialogue as a healing process for the victims of affect dysregulation in their early years. Another powerful source of information pointing to integration derives from psychotherapy outcome research which has looked at what factors make for effective therapeutic change.

There does appear to be a particular tension that emerges from the clinical literature on integration which can be summed up as follows.

Are there going to be as many assimilative approaches as there are therapists or is there gradually going to be one meta-model based on common factors based in theory and research that will give theoretical and clinical unity to the field of integration? It may be that in reality many practitioners combine aspects of these two different approaches to integration as they gradually evolve their own personal style of working, which involves a blend of both assimilation and common factors as integrative processes. The following chapter (Chapter 3) looks at the contribution of psychotherapy outcome research to the debate about integration.

3 A basis in psychotherapy outcome studies supports an integrative model

We decided to start the discussion of outcome research here with Paul's memorable question posed in 1967: 'In all its complexity, the question towards which all outcome research should ultimately be directed is the following: What treatment, by whom, is most effective for this individual with that specific problem, and under which set of circumstances?' (Paul, 1967, p. 111). The trend suggested by this question is the comparison of differential treatments or methods to ascertain what particular modality or approach and orientation is most successful with a particular problem presentation and/or client group. This has been the thrust of much outcome research in psychotherapy where rival approaches have vied with one another to prove that they have an edge on another with a particular 'condition' such as phobias or anxiety syndromes. We believe that research about the differential superiority of a particular approach may well appeal to that part in all of us that would like to see our own approach to psychotherapy proved to have an edge over all others!

We shall trace some of the main highlights in outcome research over the past circa twenty-five years since Paul's question was first posed to establish what may have been learnt to support the integrative psychotherapist. It was in 1936 that Rozenweig first talked of 'implicit common factors in diverse methods of psychotherapy' and listed such factors as the personality of the therapist; the provision for clients of an alternative way of looking at things and the systemic nature of the change process, (different orientations may differ in focus but all achieve change). In 1975 Luborsky *et al.* undertook a meta-analytic study of more than a hundred research projects that had been conducted between 1949 and 1974, all focusing on possible differential effects either between one approach to therapy and another, or between medication and therapy, or between one mode (group therapy) and another (individual). They hoped to find some consensus amongst these many studies and in their study they used a grading system involving inter alia, criteria such as adequate sample size, each compared treatment being given in equal amounts (length and frequency), and treatment outcome being evaluated by independent measures, to 'weed out the worst studies' (Luborsky et al., 1975, p. 999). They point out that the field of controlled comparative treatment research got off to start only in the mid-1950s when it was already clear from earlier research that therapy as such was better than no intervention at all. From their meta-analysis into the effectiveness of psychotherapy, they found that there was no significant difference between different types of therapy in terms of the patients improving; and that people who go through any of the different therapies that have been researched, appeared to have improved from their experience. They therefore, concluded that 'we can reach a "dodo bird verdict" – it is usually true that everybody has won and all must have prizes' (Luborsky et al., 1975, p. 1003). So the studies did not produce any clear-cut winner when psychotherapies were compared with each other; all researched forms were effective in helping clients, but no single one was superior to another.

This meta-analytic study led some people to focus on common factors amongst therapies, particularly as a basis for integration. Additional support was supplied when, in 1977 Smith and Glass also conducted a meta-analytic study which confirmed the 'Dodo bird verdict.' They concluded that: 'Despite volumes devoted to the theoretical differences among different schools of psychotherapy, the results of research demonstrate negligible differences in the effects produced by different therapy types' (Smith and Glass, 1977, p. 33) so that all methods of therapy when competently used may be regarded as equally effective. The question remained, do effective therapies perhaps have more in common with one another than was at first thought?

Bordin, E. S. (1979) in a review of the working alliance concept, pointed to the client–therapist relationship as the 'most promising of the common elements for future investigation' and Wolfe and Goldfried (1988) in a paper focused on research into integration supporting in the main a common-factors approach, referred to the therapeutic alliance as 'the quintessential integrative variable because its importance does not lie within the specifications of one school of thought' (Wolfe and Goldfried, op. cit., p. 449).

The early research projects and the meta-analyzes quoted earlier were heavily criticized, mainly on the basis of methodological inadequacies. It was believed that better sampling procedures, improved outcome measures and refined statistical techniques would indeed support differential outcomes. In many ways, this was fair comment and over the years there has been a growing sophistication in outcome research in all these and other areas. Added to this argument there was the contention that many forms of therapy have become much more sophisticated and refined over the years and more able to produce superior results in specified problem areas. Researchers continued with the endeavour to establish differential effects between therapies and as Wampold *et al.* sum this up in their article in 1997, 'the race has been run over and over again' (1997, p. 203) in the intervening years.

Overall, there remained another related issue: certain types of therapy have been privileged in being much researched, whereas others have not been. This means that we cannot necessarily come to research conclusions, either positively or negatively, about therapies that have never been touched by the researchers, yet might be respected for their effectiveness by clinicians!

The effort to prove the differential superiority of certain methods continued. With more sophisticated research methods, came the use of manuals in research to ensure similarity of delivery, but of course some forms of therapy such as behaviour therapy are easier to manualize than others such as existential therapy, which, because of its emphasis upon the uniqueness of each encounter would not be open to this form of research! This means that certain approaches will fit better into such a research paradigm, and that we may need quite another research method geared to the nature of the particular therapy to deal with approaches such as gestalt therapy, existential therapy or dialogic therapy where there is more focus on the immediacy of the here-and-now encounter, than on strategies, techniques or home work assignments.

The challenge to undertake another meta-analytic study of the outcome research projects conducted since 1975 was taken up by Wampold *et al.* in 1997; they were able to review studies which were much more sophisticated methodologically. They embarked on ambitious and careful meta-analysis of research studies published between 1970 and 1995, the period that includes Generation III research involving clinical trials (Wolfe and Goldfried, 1996). Generation III research compared different treatments for particular clinical problems, using a clinical trials model akin to that used in medical research. 'Further reflecting the shift towards the medical model, the methodology constituting the most recent approach to psychotherapy outcome research involves the DSM diagnoses, particularly on Axis I' (Goldfried and Wolfe, 1996, p. 1009).

Wampold and his colleagues conclude as follows from their meta-analysis: 'The preponderance of effects were near zero, and the frequency of larger effects was consistent with what would be produced by chance, given the sampling distribution effect sizes' (Wampold, 2001, p. 94). So in essence they made a similar finding to Luborsky and his associates 25 years before. Interestingly enough, the year in which the study was conducted did not make a significant difference to the findings, suggesting that the more sophisticated research methods were simply supporting the same outcome: 'In all, the findings are entirely consistent with the Dodo bird conjecture' (Wampold *et al.*, 1997, p. 210).

In an attempt to elucidate on the debate, Wampold (2001) discusses the effects in research of allegiance and adherence and how these processes may relate to (and confound) outcomes. Allegiance refers to the degree to which the therapist delivering the treatment believes that the particular therapeutic approach is efficacious. Adherence refers to the extent to which the therapist adhered to the interventions in the manual (or deviated from these). In earlier studies allegiance effects were ignored; but as Wampold points out in studies relating to depression where Beck's cognitive therapy was 'proved to be' superior, this effect may well be due to allegiance since these comparative studies were all carried out by adherents of cognitive therapy. Referring to his work with his colleagues, Wampold concludes: 'This meta-analysis indicated that there were no treatment differences that cannot be explained by the allegiance of the researcher' (Wampold, 2001, p. 101). Since the effects due to allegiance account for dramatically more of the variance in outcome than does the particular type of therapy, this suggests that the therapist's attitude towards the type of therapy is a critical component of effective therapy (Wampold op. cit., p. 168). What needs to be clarified here, is that the same person may often deliver two different types of therapy in these research projects, one to which he has an allegiance and another to which he is comparing his own approach.

Adherence is another fascinating area! Strict adherence to the manual in clinical trials yields interesting findings which suggest that adherence may actually be counterproductive! In referring to research in this domain Wampold summarizes thus: 'This finding hints at the fact that adherence may have detrimental effects because it suppresses the effect of competence. As measured, competence becomes a predictor of outcome only if adherence is removed' (op. cit., p. 176). Such findings are interesting to the integrative psychotherapist since they may well suggest that it is the personality of the therapist, the individual style and the ability to form a good working alliance and the client's attitude to therapy that could be central to effective therapy rather than specific techniques.

Despite the compelling evidence presented to date to the contrary, researchers appear to continue to put renewed energy into proving the effectiveness of particular approaches over others. We may well ask why? Fishman (1999) makes the point that despite the fact that research shows that specific techniques and approaches do not contribute significantly to outcome, over 80 per cent of research is still devoted to specific techniques and procedures. It seems that people are very reluctant to let go of the belief in specific approaches and accept that there may be healing factors common to all therapies.

For us, this raises the question: Would it not be better to focus on those common factors that make for change in psychotherapy? And the interesting additional questions: How does such change occur? What is the nature of the change that occurs in psychotherapy? Answers to these questions would provide interesting information for the integrative psychotherapist in practice.

So over the years, the research seems more and more to support a common or general effects hypothesis rather than the efficacy of specific differential effects; although researchers continue to try to disprove these findings. Bohart (2000) suggests that the resistance to the 'Dodo bird verdict' comes from the threat it poses for specific theories: '... if it were not so threatening ... it would long ago have been accepted as one of psychology's major findings. Then it would have been built upon and explored instead of continually being debated. The data call for a change in how we view therapy, but the field continues to stick to the old technique-focused paradigm' (Bohart, 2000, p. 129).

The influence of the medical model is still very much present in Generation III outcome research because of the shift to standardizing treatments in the mental health professions. The shift is due to the belief that models and techniques can be specified for particular conditions which leads to the development of specific protocols for the treatment of different types of problems. This move to standardize practice in psychotherapy is based on the assumption that the therapist's technical operations are responsible for client improvement rather than the quality of the relationship or other 'general' factors. In such a paradigm the 'cause' is diagnosed and then the appropriate treatment is applied in the required 'dose': in other words, the 'independent variable' (the treatment) is applied to the 'dependent variable' (the client's condition) and the effects are measured. The power of the healing is seen as coming primarily from the intervention, not from the therapeutic relationship which is kept 'the same' across treatments by the use of a standarized manual. In these 'empirically supported treatments' the therapeutic relationship, to use Goldfried's metaphor (1995a), would at best be an anaesthetic designed to prepare the client to accept and comply with the treatment. If this paradigm holds, then there should be 'best' treatments for specific disorders; as we have outlined earlier, this appears to be generally unsupported by outcome research except in very circumscribed areas. In fact, the quality of the therapeutic relationship continues to be the best predictor of successful outcome.

The research into change in psychotherapy was summarized by Lambert and Arnold (1987) in the form of a pie chart which shows that only 15 per cent of therapeutic change can be attributed to specific factors, whereas 30 per cent appears due to common factors across therapies: factors such as empathy, warmth and acceptance. As much as 40 per cent appears due to extra therapeutic change factors, such as unrelated changes in the client's life, and 15 per cent to the placebo effects. Wampold (2001) puts specific effects as low as 8 per cent and general effects at 70 per cent with an unexplained variance of 22 per cent (not specific effects). Hubble *et al.* (2000) point out that 'the empirical evidence of the impact of relationship factors in psychotherapy is substantial. These factors play a significant part in psychotherapeutic change and outcome' (op. cit., p. 37). In chapter 5 of their book, Bachelor and Horvath give a compelling review of the research into the effectiveness of the therapeutic relationship as a central vehicle for change supporting the contention of Wolfe and Goldfried that this has so far emerged as 'the quintessential integrative variable' (1988, p. 449). Bachelor and Horvath sum up as follows: 'major reviews of the psychotherapy literature have documented the significant impact on outcome of the therapeutic relationship, or of related constructs such as "therapeutic bond", in a variety of treatment environments and across a range of client problems' (In Hubble *et al.*, 2000).

To replace the medical model Wampold (2001) makes a plea for a contextual model in which he would advise the client to choose the most competent therapist available, who also practices an approach to therapy that accords with the client's world view. He believes that it is critically important that the therapy be in accord with the client's attitudes, values and culture. Such contextual sensitivity would place an emphasis on the 'match' between therapist and client and an equal emphasis on the co-construction of the therapeutic relationship by both therapist and client. Wampold suggests that clinicians need research that is focused on the context in which they work: 'the contextual model therapist understands that it is the healing context and the meaning that the client gives the experience that are important' (Wampold, 2001, p. 210).

Bovasso *et al.* (1999) conducted a study into the long-term effectiveness of therapy in a mental health service in Baltimore with a fifteen-year follow-up. The sample was a cohort of individuals with psychiatric problems randomly sampled from a community population and treated in the community. They concluded that therapy was effective and group therapy marginally more so: 'The results here suggest that psychotherapy produces changes of greater magnitude than has been previously found, which might take a long time to manifest' (op. cit., p. 537). Ramsay (quoted by Bovasso *et al.*, 1999) suggests that we need more research that is focused on 'free range humans', the people that clinicians actually meet in their consulting rooms, rather than very specially selected groups (often students at Universities), where the research is being conducted. This accords with Goldfried and Wolfe (1996) who discuss the extent to which there has been a 'strained alliance' between researchers and clinicians who live in very different worlds. They make a case for research to begin to address more closely the actual concerns of the clinician in his consulting room 'that allows us to generalize our findings more faithfully to what is needed clinically' (op. cit., p. 1015).

Bohart suggests that perhaps the most plausible explanation for the recurrent research results stressing common factors may well lie in the person of the client. 'The healing force in therapy primarily comes from the dependent variable side of the equation – the client' (Bohart, 2000, p. 132). Hubble *et al.* (2000) also maintain that the client's contribution to therapy is the neglected factor in outcome research and as this is gradually being honoured more, so is the outdated clinical view of 'therapy clients' undergoing change from 'slow-witted plodders (or pathological monsters) to resourceful, motivated hunters of more satisfying lives' (Hubble *et al.*, 2000, p. 425). In this shift of emphasis, the client is taking centre stage rather than therapist or his theories! These writers point out that research into therapy outcomes has consistently focused on therapist provision rather than on what the client brings to the relationship. Even the early research into client-centered therapy highlighted the therapist provision of 'core conditions' that were considered essential to creating a facilitating environment with little emphasis on what the client contributed.

Hubble *et al.* (2000) wryly quote an African proverb to underline their point: 'Until lions have their historians, tales of the hunt shall always glorify the hunter!'

Hubble *et al.* (2000) trenchantly sum up this new focus: 'We believe the Dodo verdict occurs because the client's abilities to use whatever is offered surpass any differences that might exist in techniques or approaches' (Hubble *et al.*, 2000, p. 95). This view of the client as resourceful and as the primary architect of his own change stresses the naturally occurring healing processes in therapy. Since different therapies each provide some useful structure or tools for solving personal problems, it is likely that the client creatively uses what is on offer. In this sense different therapies provide different structures or scaffoldings for the learning process that forms the heart of therapy; the menu from which the client selects what suits his palate. It is perhaps the client who is most resourceful, rather than the therapist!! These writers suggest that research in this area supports the belief that the more the therapist's rationale fits the client's implicit models of how problems are solved in his culture, and the more the procedure includes active engagement in a task which challenges him, the more likely the client will have hope in the procedure and benefit from the process. They maintain that a more collaborative model is indicated which would facilitate interpersonal dialogue as the context for learning. This brings them very much in line with Wampold's (2001) contextual model described earlier.

The authors of this book find themselves aligned with these positions; honouring the client's view of the change process; honouring the co-creation of the therapeutic relationship as the vehicle and context for change; and being sensitive to the contextual demands of the situation in which therapy takes place. This leads to a central respect for the client's model of the change process; a respect for the client's informal theory about the problem and the change process; and a respect for the client's beliefs in the credibility of the particular therapeutic process. Even if a treatment has demonstrated its efficacy, the client may still view it with suspicion as perhaps unfair or harsh! What is vital is that the client is open to using what is offered and finds the approach acceptable and palatable!

Part 2
Theoretical underpinnings

4 A developmental–relational model for integration

A multidimensional view of self functions

A key theme in our approach to integration is a focus on the developing self. In this chapter we review the different aspects of self-in-relationship as we believe that change in psychotherapy can occur in one or several or all of these areas. At a given point in time for any client certain of these areas will be more focal than others, and at different life stages others may come into focus. We also see that these areas of self experience are inevitably interrelated but find it useful to focus on them separately to highlight certain unique aspects of our self experience:

- the biological: relationship of self to body
- the intrapsychic: relationship of self to self
- the interpersonal: relationship of self to others
- the intercultural: relationship to culture, race, nation, business world, wider context
- the ecological: relationship of self to nature
- the transcendental: relationship of self to the transcendent

The biological: relationship of self to body

The concept of the body image is a frequent focus in psychotherapy and underpins a person's self concept in a fundamental way that can influence all aspects of the person's functioning. We prefer to use the term 'the body self' (Krueger, 1989) to refer to the person's experience of the embodied self, including all their kinesthetic experiences of external and internal bodily aspects and processes. Susie Orbach entitled her recent Bowlby memorial lecture 'There is no such thing as a body.' In her reference to Winnicott's famous statement, she emphasizes the importance of the mother–child relationship in the development of the child's sense of her bodily self (Orbach, 2003). The (m)other is centrally important in attuning to the child and affirming the newborn in her sense of bodily self. We are also aware of the importance of honouring here the cultural context in which this process is located since there are many subtle differences in the handling of children across cultures and in attitudes to the body and bodily processes which the child will internalize. Clemmens and Bursztyn (2003) point out that as therapists we need to be aware of any 'assumptions about physical movement, expression and structure' (p. 18) that relate to body/culture. We can easily assume that a person shares our own experience and end up pathologizing a response that reflects cultural origin rather than dysfunction. For those of us who have moved from cultures that are highly tactile into cultures where touch is sparingly used, an awareness of this difference will be essential to effective practice.

The development of the body self is intimately dependent on a delicate process of attunement between the (m)other and the child. The intersubjective nature of this process of attunement is at the heart of the child's experience of self as a body self reflected in the responsive resonance of the other. Through touching, stroking and handling the child's body the mother conveys to the child on a sensory level a sense of his bodily self and its boundaries. 'Our self is first and foremost a body-as-experienced-being-handled-and-held-by-other self, in other words, our self is first and foremost a body-in-relation-self' (Aron and Anderson, 1998, p. 20). The intersubjective nature of this process is well documented by child researchers such as Stern (1985), Beebe and Lachmann (1998), inter alia. It is the quality of attunement on the part of the parent that will influence child's subsequent acceptance of, and loving attitude to, his own body or result in a rough non-acceptance, a dissociative distancing or an outright loathing of his physical self.

One of the authors has a vivid memory of working with a client who was focusing on her experience of her body; at a certain point, she started tugging at the skin on her upper arm. The therapist drew her attention to this and commented on the roughness of her touch. At that moment, she recovered a memory of her mother bathing her as a child: 'She used to tug at me and handle me roughly ... I can still feel the discomfort of her touch ... but that was all there was ... she never hugged me or stroked me gently ... this was all I knew.' We internalize the manner in which we are handled and responded to which informs our bodily self experience and our body image. As our early experiences of touch and attunement/misattunement occurs at a non-verbal stage of development, these memories are stored as bodily memories with no conscious verbal access. These experiences constitute our body memory which is usually accessed by sensory cues outside the realm of conscious verbal autobiograhical memory. These may take the form of kinesthetic, olfactory or visual flashbacks to earlier experiences and contribute to a sense of well-being or to a sense of feeling uncomfortable or 'not at home' in our bodies. The accuracy of the (m)other's early attunement is crucial to the child's development of an integrated body self. 'The mother's resonance with the infant's experience provides him with a "mirror" that reinforces and affirms the infant's sense of existence' (Krueger, 1989, p. 6).

Of course, it is not only through physical touch that our body self is informed; it is through all our senses that we internalize the responses of the other to our embodied selves. Trevarthen (1998) has demonstrated how the parent can respond delicately to the rhythms of the baby through sounds and movements that reflect the 'music' of the child's inner rhythmical pacing and so convey a sense of attunement that matches the child's process. In watching his film footage, it is possible to see this delicate process of attunement in action and witness the child's delight at the parent's sensitivity (Trevarthen, 1998). Stern (1985) has discussed research into the handling of children by their mothers which suggests that when a depressed mother handles her baby she may do this in a functional manner attending to the necessary duties, but her touch lacks any vitality and warmth. This process leads to a 'depressed mood' in the child as well. Stern's concepts of the 'vitality affects' seems very relevant here: these refer to the quality of the mother's sensory responses, like the tone and intensity of her speech, the firmness of her touch, the timbre of her voice, all of which convey to the child a sense of her involvement and attunement to the child. Vitality affects can be conveyed in 'how the mother picks up baby, folds the diapers, grooms her hair or the baby's hair, reaches for the bottle, unbuttons her blouse' (Stern, 1985, p. 54). The child will sense the energy and lovingness in her handling of and responses to him and we believe that much of what is later described as 'body image' is formed through this early process of interactive communication at this non-verbal level between parent and child. Stern's focus on mutimodal matching is also of relevance here since the music of the mother's voice may convey loving touch; it is through all the senses that the child absorbs the attuned responses of the other.

The caretaker's attitude to the child's bodily self will, therefore, be conveyed through the quality of this early mirroring. Where the parent is herself ashamed at her own basic bodily processes, she may transmit this shame in her handling of the child: '... if there is overstimulation or understimulation, body self distortions or nonformations begin, and may later result in narcissistic disturbances' (Krueger, 1989, p. 6). If shame becomes associated with basic bodily processes, this may spill over to affect the person's self image in other areas of functioning and also prevent an effective integration of body, emotions and mind. In extreme cases, this may result in dissociative processes where the person feels severely alienated from her own sensory, emotional and bodily experience. Shame is particularly relevant in cases of physical and/or sexual abuse or where the child is physically different to other children and is shamed in the process of growing up.

The intrapsychic: relationship of self to self

Recent literature on self-development has begun to focus on the relationship of self-as-subject to the self-as-object (Aron and Anderson, 1998; Fonaghy *et al.*, 2002). The self as subject refers to the 'I' who observes, organizes and interprets my experience and constructs the 'me' as my self-concept, my mental representation of myself as I operate in the world, a view of myself as an object amongst other objects (Fonaghy *et al.*, 2002). Aron in referring back to James' distinction between the 'I' and the 'Me', describes the 'me' as referring to 'the person's self-concept, all that a person can know about oneself through one's own observations or through feedback from others ... the more objective aspect of self' (Aron, 1998, p. 5). The 'I' refers to the 'self-as-knower', the self-as-subject, the self-as-agent (Aron, op. cit.). Much of the psychological literature on the self concept that a person develops has focused on the self-as-object, on how I perceive myself amongst others and the values and qualities that I attribute to myself, my appearance and my behaviour. Less attention has been paid to the self-as-knower, the self as the subject or organizer of experience. Fonaghy *et al.* (2002) in exploring the development of the 'reflective process' in the growing child have looked at how a child develops a 'theory of mind', and a sense of being an 'I' in relation to the 'I' of the other (2002, p. 24). Kohut, too, has placed the self centrally in his theory as the supraordinate organizer of experience dedicated to preserving a coherent sense of self (Kohut, 1977). He saw this sense of self as innate to the person, albeit in a rudimentary form, which then requires effective responsiveness from others in the environment to develop fully.

Both Aron (1998) and Fonaghy *et al.* (2002) have discussed at length the crucial significance of the reflective function, which lies at the heart to our construction of self. Aron defines self-reflexivity as 'the capacity to experience, observe and reflect on oneself as both a subject and an object'. He sees this dialectical process of experiencing oneself as a subject as well as being able to reflect on oneself as an object as an integrated intellectual, experiential and affective process (Aron, 1998, pp. 3–4). In this sense we see it as deeply rooted in our phenomenological experience of self-in-the-world. We need as therapists to be sensitive to the context, the field of the person's experience as this is boundaried by family, peers and wider cultural milieu. In effective functioning, a person can dialogue fluidly between these two polarities of the self as subject and the self as object and has developed the 'mental capacity to move back and forth, and to maintain the tension, between a view of the self as a subject and a view of the self as an object' (Aron, op. cit., p. 5).

Pathology may be viewed as the inability to maintain a creative tension between these polarities of the self and to settle at one extreme or the other. For example, an overemphasis of the 'I' at the expense of the 'Me' may mean that the person's focus is entirely on the subjective with no capacity to view themselves as an object among other objects, a narcissistic grandiosity with an overemphasis on self which ignores the needs of others. An overemphasis on the 'Me' may leave a person feeling that she has no sense of self, a sense of being adrift in a world of others, an experience of a void where self would be. The depressive, for example, may become fixed in the 'Me' polarity and lose all capacity to view self-as-subject, seeing themselves as just another object in a world of objects. Getting polarized at one of these extremes leads to interpersonal inflexibility and a lack of movement that results in pathology. In healthy functioning, people have the capacity to move fluidly between these polarities and retain both a sense of self-worth and self-agency alongside a sense of being one amongst others.

Wright's (1991) concept of a third-person perspective is of relevance here. At first the child is entirely dependent on the mother to reflect back to him what she sees. This view may be positive and affirming of his sense of self, but it may also be misattuned or openly hostile or rejecting, so shaping the child's self-concept in particular ways. What is introduced by the father (or another significant other) is the possibility of another perspective, which he calls the 'third person perspective'. This at best offsets the original reflection on himself that the child has received. This third-person perspective provides another view of what is happening, and another view of the 'self' of the child in relation to others and the world. The child's experience of the self with mother/primary carer is now part of a larger field in which the child is no longer the centre of attention, but part of a larger interdependent world of people and objects that affect one another reciprocally 'taking the view of the third person makes possible for the first time an appreciation of a subject's position within an interactive behavioural system' (Wright, 1991, p. 234). This capacity to appreciate multiple points of view for us refers to the capacity to view self-as-subject and self-as-object in a moving context of relationships with other people. This relates closely to Buber's concept of inclusion, the capacity to be in touch with myself, to empathize with the other, and to hold a metaperspective on this process (Buber, 1923/96). The capacity for inclusion we would regard as an important facet of metacognitive processing and the ability that underlies the capacity of the self-as-knower to develop a theory of mind that encompasses a view of subject-to-subject relating.

Ogden (1994) makes a significant contribution to this dis cussion by stressing the importance of the creation of metaphor by the 'I' in describing the 'Me' of my self experi- ence; it is these metaphors that enable the 'Me' to emerge from invisibility so that 'I can see myself'. Many of the ways in which people describe their view of themselves are based on some type of imagery, for example, 'I am a mover and shaker' or 'I am a mere shadow on life's stage'. Such images involve a view of the self from the eye ('I') of the observer. Psychological terms may also be of this kind, for example, referring to my 'inner child' (Berne, 1961) as a part of myself with which I have a relationship, from the vantage point of the 'I', the self-as-subject.

The interpersonal: the relationship of self to others

We view relationships from an intersubjective perspective; there is an ongoing process of 'reciprocal mutual influence' (Stolorow and Atwood, 1992, p. 18) at work in all relating that leads to a constant interflow of shared experience. As babies, we all develop a characteristic attachment style in our interaction with primary carers so well described in the work on attachment styles (Holmes, 1993). Our style of approach- ing others, whether secure or insecure, lays the foundation for our contact style (Wheeler, 1991) that will gradually evolve as our way of approaching others and construing the world. We find helpful in this regard the ideas of Wheeler (1991) enlarged upon by Mackewn (1997, p. 28) that all contact functions have two polarities, for example, 'confluence ... isolation' and each person will find a place of 'comfort' along each continuum. To follow the above example, for some of us our contact will involve a tendency to remain at the confluence end of this polarity, in an effort to merge or become symbiotic with the other; for others of us we will tend to maintain a sense of isolation or distance from the other. Developing a flexibility along this and other of these polarities will provide us with a wider range of options in our relationships. The constellation of our particular contact functions will be informed by our attachment style and also subsequently shape our personality style.

We accept that the reflective function, the ability to understand the states of mind of the other so well outlined by Fonaghy *et al.* (2002) is of critical importance in making possible constructive mutual interaction with others. In developing the capacity to 'read' the minds of others, children are able to appreciate the 'beliefs, feelings, attitudes, desires, hopes, knowledge, imagination, pretense, deceit, intentions, plans ...' (Fonaghy *et al.*, p. 24) of the people they meet. This awareness of the states of mind of those around them assists children in building up an internal mental representation of self-and-other that forms the basis of interpersonal relating. The reflection function as defined by Fonaghy *et al.* (op. cit.) involves intellectual, emotional and imaginative components in interaction with one another.

Aron and Sommer-Anderson (1998, p. 10) makes the telling point that 'this capacity for metacognitive processing, or reflective self-awareness, has been found to be even more significant in determining health and pathology than is the quality of the attachment experiences that are remembered'. It is from the failure of this capacity for mentalization and reflective function to develop when it is undermined by trauma and developmental derailments such as affect dysregulation that pathology results. A failure to manage mental states may lead a person to enact what she is unable to represent and result, inter alia, in self harm, somatic symptoms or 'acting out behaviours'.

As discussed earlier, the self has two dimensions 'self as subject' and 'self as object', the I and the Me, which are in a constant dynamic interaction. The work of Fonaghy *et al.* (2002) has contributed significantly to our understanding of the 'I', whereas we draw from other sources for an understanding of how the self-concept, the 'me' of our interrelational experience develops. Kohut (1978, p. 60) has given us a view of the use of the significant other as a 'self–object', of our capacity to experience ourselves in the mind of another as a means for building up our own sense of self integrity. His discussion of the 'self–object transferences' which develop in therapy and offer the person a 'second chance' to repair developmental deficits is the person's way of gaining support for the development of a sound sense of self (Kohut, op. cit.). The 'mirroring' transference provides the person with a reflection of his own sense of narcissistic importance and derives from 'the child self that actively seeks out and expects an alive, bright-eyed, engaged parent' and sees himself reflected in the gaze of that parent (Tolpin, 1997, p. 6). The 'idealizing self–object transference' reflects a need to hold the other as an object of admiration and is reflective of the child's need to idealize the parent: 'You're great, what you are and what you do is great; you belong to me, I belong to you, therefore I'm great too' (Tolpin, op. cit.). The twinship self-object transference reflects a person's need to be like the other and provides a sense of belonging and kindred experiences: 'We're alike, we're in step with each other, we're both great when we're together' (Tolpin, op. cit.). Kohut's later emphasis on mature self–object needs make clear that he considers the meeting of self–object needs through interaction with others a lifelong process (Kohut, 1984). We draw from our close relationships, from our friendships and our collegial and social interactions, ongoing nourishment for our sense of self. They reflect back to us facets of ourselves that support our self-concepts.

Object relations theories have contributed an understanding of how we internalize our interpersonal relationships so that these become part of our own mental life and provide the material for our intrapsychic dialogues as well as the patterns of our interpersonal relating. In getting an appreciation of the 'Me' of our self dimensions, we have found the transactional analysis concepts of 'Parent, Adult and Child ego states' particularly helpful (Berne, 1961). The 'Parent' represents the internalized figures of influence in our early lives and forms part of our own repertoire of self expression. We may unconsciously behave and sound like one of our parents in our interactions with others as we slip into a parent-ego state. This expression may or may not be acceptable to us as a desired part of our self-concept. When we regress into a mode of expression that was part of our own historical experience of self, we are in a child-ego state. This again may occur in or outside of conscious awareness and may or may not be an appropriate or relevant response to the present situation. If we revert to a traumatized child-ego state under external pressure, we may lose all sense of the present context and relive the original experience with all its intensity. This process of getting caught up in our own internal world and the loss of the sense of present context seems close to what Fonaghy *et al.* (2002, p. 56) refer to as 'psychic equivalence'. The adult-ego state refers to our capacity to respond to the here-and-now of experience, to respond appropriately in the present context to the other. These three categories of response reflect different aspects of my experience of me-in-relation-to-the-other, some of them feeling closer to my experience of true self and others less congruent with my self-concept and therefore more remote from my 'real or true' self-experience.

Assagioli's (1965) view of sub-personalities provides another interesting perspective on the self-concept, the me of my self-experience, as I adopt different roles and relationship stances in response to different people and circumstances in my life. I may have a 'teacher self', a 'fun-loving party self', 'a serious reflective self' and so on, all of which contribute to the multiplicity of facets of my self-concept. The 'I' of my self experience will reflect upon and hold a view of these sub-selves. Polster (1995) describes us as possessing a 'population of selves' all of which are potential possibilities when we interact with others; I can choose the 'member' of the population that I wish to infuse with energy at a particular time. These facets of self develop in our interactions with different people and contexts in our lives and become part of the population of our internal world which can be 'animated' in our intercourse with others (Polster, 1995, p. 10). Our senses of self are developed in relation to family, peer groups, people in authority, colleagues and change in dynamic interaction with others throughout our lives. The self is always a self-in-relationship to others.

The intercultural dimension: relationship of self to culture, race, social and political context

Eleftheriadou (1994) defines culture as 'a way of creating shared ways of functioning in order to communicate effectively', including 'shared events, practices, roles, values, myths, beliefs, habits, symbols, illusions and realities'. Culture, he maintains, exists inside people (psychologically) and outside (in the existing social institutions). Culture is not a closed system but changes with each generation.

Other authorities have also adopted such a broad definition of culture that includes, disability, age, religion, political affiliation, gender, sexual orientation, class, status, race and ethnicity (see Bernard, 1994; Ridley, 1995; Pederson, 1997). Such a comprehensive understanding of culture recognizes people in their complexity and better equips therapists to deal with complex differences within and between cultural groups. In an earlier publication Gilbert and Evans (2000), argued that psychotherapy theories were culturally encapsulated and lacked awareness of multicultural issues. In a similar vein Krause (1998, p. A) writes 'Culture cannot be accessed sufficiently through the narrow personal relationship between the psychotherapist and the individual client ... especially not if the cultural background of the therapist and client are markedly different.' Andrew Samuels has also written '... depth psychology must face the problem that it is not possible to depict a person divorced from his or her cultural, social, gender, ethnic, and above all, economic and ecological contexts'. (Samuels, A., 1993).

The clear implication of this is that integrative psychotherapy (and psychotherapy in general) needs to question its assumptions about the therapeutic process and the relevance of models of psychotherapy it integrates into its frame in order to respond effectively to clients from different cultures and contexts. Ridley (1995) claims that many psychotherapists are unaware of the assumptions of the interpretations of their models in perpetuating racism.

We believe ignorance is the major factor in the perpetuation of oppressive practice in psychotherapy and is supported by a complacency borne of the fact that the profession of psychotherapy occupies a privileged and powerful position, operating from dominant normative models and assumptions that appear to have been largely unquestioned. Espin and Gawalek (1992) hold that 'theories of psychotherapy have been notorious for their neglect of cultural variability as well as gender issues. Most psychological theory is anglo-saxon in its perspective and conception of human nature.' Do each of the purportedly 480 schools of psychotherapy really rest upon separate and self-contained bodies of knowledge each conveying the impression that it represents the 'truth' of psychotherapy? (Karuso, quoted in Dryden and Norcross, 1990).

The integrative therapist is not a detached observer but works with an attitude of horizontality, attempting to avoid hierarchies in description of behaviour. According to Eleftheriadou the therapist 'needs to aspire to equality where he/she both explores clients feeling towards people of different race and culture and includes the ability to accept from clients from ethnic minorities distrust and anger toward the majority culture' (Eleftheriadou, 1994, p. 34). This attitude of equalization is compatible with the dialogical approach which requires an appreciation of difference in order to facilitate true contact (Evans, 1996).

From our perspective on integrative psychotherapy we, therefore, appreciate the notion of consensus put forward by Varela et al., that human beings create consensually agreed constructions of reality. A person creates his or her world moment by moment but requires the existence of an other to do so, in co-dependent origination. The image of Varela et al. is of the 'path created in walking' (Varela et al., 1993). We also agree with Eleftheriadou's helpful distinction between a 'cross cultural' approach and a 'trans cultural' approach. The former implies the use of our own self-reference to understand another person, while the latter emphasizes the need 'to walk beyond cultural difference' (Eleftheriadou, 1994, p. 31).

The integrative psychotherapist, supported by the phenomenological basis of integrative psychotherapy, adopts a stance whereby all phenomena are accepted as 'normal', as a person's subjective reality. Thus the integrative psychotherapist may transcend culture by honouring the unique world view and values of the client and consequently allow cultural issues to influence the process and direction of the therapeutic work. Integrative psychotherapy is also informed by holism which enables the therapist to see the client in the wholeness of the totality of their life situation. Essentially then we believe that every client can only be understood from their own frame of reference, and from within their own cultural milicu.

Finally we would argue that integrative psychotherapy in refusing to be constrained by a single psychotherapeutic orientation works towards what Ridley refers to as an 'ideographic perspective' which is trans theoretical (Ridley, 1995, pp. 82–3).

This extension of Buber's I–Thou attitude to the client's cultural background supports a deeper level of contact with the client than if we were to ignore the context within which and out of which their lives emerge. We also maintain that this attitude of I–Thou needs to be extended towards the natural world in which we live. King asks the challenging question, 'What is the point in liberating people if the planet cannot sustain liberated lives' (King, 1990, p. 121).

The ecological dimension: the self in relation to nature, the world around us

Environmental catastrophe is upon us in the form of global warming, depletion of the ozone, air pollution, water pollution, deforestation, overpopulation, and the extinction of thousands of species (Howard, 1997). The current paradigm of the western psychology is that of development where growth is seen as 'more', and self is largely understood as 'consumer'. 'It assumes an enduring progression by which individuals, organizations and nations consume matter and information from its environment and progresses to a state better and grander than what it has known before. Without a qualitative measure of what is better we have relied on quantity, more wealth, more consumption' Pilisuk (2001). Ironically humanistic psychology's emphasis on 'self realization' has unwittingly placed human needs above all else, including nature (Kuhn, 2001).

Psychologists are in the front line in hearing the voices of people victimized by the pressures towards personal and technical development. We see them as anxious, pressurized by work, depressed by their disrupted relationships, failing to find meaning in a society that depicts consumption as fulfilment, struggling to cope with illness that might have been prevented, loss of control over decisions to impersonal corporate and governmental actions, and unable to gain sustenance from the beauty of nature. 'And what do psychologists do? For the most part talk to individuals in small offices about their personal development' (Pilisuk, 2001, p. 34).

From the perspective of psychotherapy in general, and integrative psychotherapy in particular we believe there is a need to challenge the dominant world view of industrialized nations. As Metzner points out, our personal and professional values should include such concerns as, sustainability, preservation and restoration of all life forms and habitats on earth, not just those of humans or one group of humans (Metzner, 1999).

Despite a general complacency within psychotherapy we are encouraged and challenged by the growing number of voices within the profession calling for the fostering of an ecological consciousness, which would require a change in our understanding of human psychology to include the human relationship with the natural world (Rozak, 1992).

A different perspective of the role of humans in the world needs to be integrated into the theory and practice of psychotherapy. Naess (1989) the founder of Deep Ecology may offer a viable perspective. He identifies the 'ecological self' and views it as a consequence of a natural psychological maturation from the ego to social self, from social self to metaphysical self, and from metaphysical self to ecological self. We would wish to emphasize these stages of evolution of the self as phases rather than stages. That is, each phase of development is taken up, but not discarded by the subsequent phase but carried forward and integrated within the ecological self and further developed in the process. So maturation would allow access to any and all phases of self-development as appropriate to the current circumstances and demands of the situation. A further integration of the notion of 'interdependence' of Pilisuk complements that of Naess's 'ecological self', and both are compatible with our extension of the 'I–Thou' attitude to the natural world. In the notion of 'interdependence' self is regarded as part of a larger clan and of a larger ecology and personal fulfilment is, in part, consequent upon the contribution to something greater than the enhancement of self. Pilisuk points to the research supporting attachment from Bowlby (1988), to Stern (1985) as stepping stones in this ecological consciousness where human development is seen as interconnection rather than growth. Pilisuk cites research that 'provides compelling evidence that resistance to breakdown in all forms of health and mental health are similarly linked to the strength of social ties and the quality of life' (Pilisuk, 2001, p. 26). As with the dimension of culture, so too the ecological dimension requires the raising of consciousness within psychotherapy, and among psychotherapists, in order to develop the capacity and ability to be able to recognize and identify and respond empathically to these dimensions of being human that have always been present but largely neglected.

Transpersonal dimension: relationship of self to the transcendent

In seeking to find meaning 'within' – through psychology, psychotherapy, art and literature, music, philosophy etc. or 'without' – through politics, social action, etc. human beings have also sought meaning 'beyond' themselves notably through religion, psychic, cultural and ecological aspects of human experience. There also appears to us an overemphasis on eastern psychology and spiritual tradition, perhaps because of the apparent impoverishment in western spirituality? We wish to explore a way through what we think is an erroneous split between the ordinary and the extraordinary, the human and the transhuman, which honours the transpersonal or spiritual dimension and at the same time 'earths' the spiritual in the concrete of our own daily existence and that of our clients. In doing so we wish to acknowledge and respect the different religious and spiritual traditions whose very difference appears to us essential to the richness and diversity of human existence. Our perspective intends to touch the 'ordinary' human dimension that appear significant in the lives of our clients and in our opinion has the seeds of the 'super ordinary'. Perhaps this may prove an ecumenical focus within psychotherapy, encouraging exploration across the different religious and spiritual traditions within the profession?

In the 1960s Maslow was among the first to identify a need for what he called the 'fourth force' in psychology. In the preface to *Towards a Psychology of Being* he wrote 'I consider humanistic third force psychology (humanistic psychology) to be transitional, a preparation for a still higher fourth force psychology, transpersonal, transhuman, centred in the cosmos rather than in human needs and interest, going beyond humanness' (Maslow, 1968). In a similar vein Victor Frankl wrote 'being human always points to something other than itself' (Frankl, 1966). Maslow dismayed many in humanistic psychology when he took transpersonal into the realm of the higher or transcendental consciousness and established the *Journal of Transpersonal Psychology*.

While Rollo may acknowledge that human beings lived in two realms or kingdoms – the natural and the spiritual – he was critical of the hierarchical structure (higher and lower) expressed in transpersonal psychology as expressed in the writings of Maslow and more recently of Ken Wilber and 'valued all that enhances the inner life of human beings' (May, 1985). We are sympathetic with the views of Chaudhuri (1975, p. 7) who maintained that 'trans personal experiences are still a specific mode of human experience' and Moustakas (1985, p. 5) who wrote, 'We consider the mystical or transpersonal as personal, as a human capacity within the scope of being human.'

While sympathetic to transpersonal psychology we regret the split between higher and lower, explicit or implicit in much of the transpersonal literature and which appears to us all too reminiscent of the dualism inherent in Judaic-Christianity between the human and divine, and body and soul. From our integrative perspective both the transpersonal and the human are essentially connected. Naess (1989) believes, and we agree, that the ecological self brings forth a relationship of unity or wholeness which embraces all life forms and has a quality of the transpersonal. However for us while the sense of interdependence and connection is essential it is also necessary to focus on the quality of contact with the other – not only the other person(s), but also with a person's cultural background as well as the natural world. Contact, within the 'I–Thou' meaning of this engagement or meeting, is characterized by depth and quality and has been described by Lynne Jacobs as the 'highest form of meeting'? What we are referring to here is that form of meeting into which each participant enters with an attitude of openness and vulnerability, not seeking to control the direction of the encounter but allowing 'the between' to influence the level of engagement and the content of the dialogue. Such engagement is not always comfortable for when there is a mutuality of contact, that is, when there is a reciprocal surrender to 'the between', then what emerges within the meeting cannot be predicted or controlled unless one or other participant leaves the encounter. To fully engage with the other requires a willingness to remain in dialogue often with uncertainty, ambiguity and not knowing. When such a way of being human is reciprocal, or mutual, then there is a possibility of contact in the deep sense that Buber conveyed in his writings. Paradoxically it is through the human encounter! meeting with an other person(s) that a sometimes numinous, mystical and extra ordinary (transpersonal) experience may occur, and not simply, or perhaps rarely in our opinion, outside of the human encounter!

In what sense is it possible to engage in I–Thou with cultural issues or with the natural world for surely neither can speak or react reciprocally in the manner that a human being may so speak? We believe profoundly that the natural world is speaking loudly and disturbingly to the way human beings are engaging with the planet. We hear and witness the response of our planet as it groans and suffers under the attack of commercial and industrial growth and exploitation, and we have examples of how our planet can respond in a nurturing and supportive way to human beings in the countless but still relatively few experiments in organic farming, alternative energy projects, cooperative trading groups which activity appear to us to work within a characteristically I–Thou frame. Similarly there are countless examples of individuals and groups working with an I–Thou attitude in culturally (and economically) deprived areas across the globe and with and between different ethnic and religious groups in the world 'trouble spots' like Northern Ireland, Palestine, Kosovo and so on. Sometimes it is necessary to sustain an I–Thou attitude until there can be a reciprocal I–Thou response. We repeat it through human engagement that the 'ordinary' can be experienced as extraordinary, the personal experienced with a quality of the transpersonal, the mundane experienced as mystical and the human experienced as divine.

One of the greatest theologians of the twentieth century Wolfhart Pannenberg maintained in his masterly work, *Jesus: God and Man* (1983), that the most significant idea in Judaic-Christian scripture was that human beings were made in the image of God. Essentially there is no distinction between humanity and divinity in the sense that to develop and grow as a human being, is to grow towards the divine image. To become fully human as God intended. To illustrate this idea we end this section with a short story, whose meaning, taken metaphorically, helps to further illustrate the significance of being human. Turgenev was sitting in a country church somewhere in Russia at the turn of the twentieth century. He sat next to a peasant whose sweat and ragged clothing stank of the farmyard. He made to move but instead was overcome with a strange and repugnant conviction that he was sitting alongside the Messiah himself. But how could this be, such an ordinary man as this? And then it came to him in a tearful awakening that just such an ordinary man was the alleged son of God.

5 The process of integrative psychotherapy and a critique of the model

The co-created psychotherapeutic relationship as a central focus

Central to our conception of psychotherapy is a focus on the co-creation of the therapeutic relationship as an interactional event in which both parties participate. It is not a one-sided relationship in which one party 'does' to the other while the other is a passive recipient, but rather a constantly evolving co-constructed relational process to which client and therapist alike contribute. It is in, and through, the co-created relationship between therapist and client, as this evolves over time, that healing and change take place. The therapeutic relationship is viewed as a dynamic process between two people in mutual interaction in the therapy room, always a unique encounter because of the individualities of the persons involved. This is very much a two-person view of the therapeutic process, acknowledging that the client too will impact on the therapist in an ongoing way.

Our approach is, therefore, very much in line with the following streams within contemporary relational psychotherapy. First, we draw on intersubjectivity theory which emphasizes the concept of 'reciprocal mutual influence' (Stolorow and Atwood, 1992, p. 18) stressing the inextricable nature of the therapeutic relationship between two people. Stolorow and Atwood (1992) succinctly summarize their position: '... our view (is) that ... the trajectory of self experience is shaped at every point in development by the intersubjective system in which it crystalizes' (p. 18). They use the term 'codetermination' to describe this reciprocal process in development and in psychotherapy (op. cit., p. 24).

Second, we are allied with contemporary dialogic approaches within gestalt therapy which focus on the healing dialogue in psychotherapy and stress the importance of the space between therapist and client as the area in which healing takes place (Hycner, 1993). '... if we take seriously the concept of the *between* there is a reality that is greater than the sum total of the experience of the therapist and the client. *Together* they form a totality that provides a context for the individual experience of both. Perhaps that is the most succinct meaning of the between' (Hycner, 1991, pp. 134–5).

We also draw from contemporary relational psychoanalysis with the central tenet, 'The relational approach that I am advancing views the patient–analyst relationship as continually established and reestablished through ongoing mutual influence in which both patient and analyst systematically affect, and are affected by, each other' (Aron, 1999, p. 248). These three contemporary relational approaches all stress the mutuality of the therapeutic process as a co-construction between the therapist and the client. We need to stress, however, that the techniques used, the therapist's use of self, views on transference and counter-transference, views on the use of self-disclosure and the manner of relating in the encounter with the client, vary widely.

Honouring uniqueness and contextual influences

The conclusion that we have gradually drawn in our studies of contemporary relational approaches to psychotherapy across the board, is that there is a gradual but slowly growing awareness of the importance of honouring the individuality and uniqueness of the person and character of the therapist. The therapist is no longer viewed as a neutral presence but as a person in his/her own right. Each of us brings our own personal history to the therapeutic encounter, our gender, our age, our ethnic origin, our race, our personality, with the particular meaning our unique constellation of qualities may evoke in the context in which we practice. 'A genuine relationship can't be established if there aren't shared meanings' (Hycner, 1991, p. 135). Both therapist and client bring to the relationship their own unique 'organizing principles' developed in the course of their own histories, which shape their perception of events (Stolorow and Atwood, 1992, p. 25), and these interface in the therapeutic encounter. The person of the therapist cannot be neutralized; she is unique and her uniqueness will influence the process.

Aron considers that patients are always 'accommodating to the interpersonal reality of the analyst's character' but may not refer directly to sensitive aspects of the analyst's presentation. Yet they 'are likely to communicate these observations only indirectly through allusions to others, as displacements, or through descriptions of these characteristics as aspects of themselves ...' (Aron, 1999, p. 251). As therapists we need to be sensitive to these oblique communications from our clients as they may be reflecting their struggle with some conscious or unconscious aspects of our own process. '... all the experience of both analysand and analyst is an intersubjective mixture. Thus, all the analyst's experiences are generated, by definition, by a commingling of psychic content from two minds' (Mitchell and Aron, 1999, p. 460).

The relational unconscious: the 'analytic third'

Ogden (1994) in speaking of the unconscious intersubjective 'analytic third' takes this concept of commingling even further and draws attention to an unconscious co-created process between therapist and client which can provide a valuable insight into the client's process. The analytic third emerges from the interplay between subjectivity and intersubjectivity which generates as it were a third presence in the room. Ogden (1994) makes the interesting point that any reveries or preoccupations on the part of the analyst during the therapeutic hour, even if they seem frivolous and distractions from the business at hand, may actually hold a meaning for the meeting. What we may usually 'bracket' off or berate ourselves for being distracted by, may relate to the analytic third and hold valuable unconscious communications about the quality of the therapeutic relationship (op. cit.).

Gerson (2004) speaks of 'a relational unconscious' that he describes as 'the unrecognized bond that wraps each relationship, infusing the expression and constriction of each partner's subjectivity and individual unconscious within that particular relationship'. The concept of the relational unconscious highlights the interconnectedness of each therapeutic dyad and forms 'an unseen bridge' between them (Gerson, 2004, pp. 72–3). This definition of the concept of the analytic third adds a further dimension to the co-creation or co-determination of relationships mentioned earlier, in that it suggests that we create our relationships reciprocally, at both conscious and unconscious levels. In a therapeutic process it is, therefore, important to be open to the messages filtering through from the shared relational unconscious. These may emerge in many forms, as dreams, as fantasies, as seeming distractions, as obsessional preoccupations, as physical symptoms or in other forms of acting out by either therapist or client. Relational psychotherapists will pay careful attention to these phenomena as possibly providing rich insights into 'stuck' places in the therapy.

The power of the counter-transference as part of the therapeutic technique

A relational therapy, such as we advocate, calls primarily for the full presence of the therapist in the room with the client with a focus on the immediacy of their encounter. The importance of empathic responsiveness is generally accepted as essential to the establishment of a firm working alliance. Rogers' emphasis on empathy (Rogers, 1951) from the humanistic tradition and Kohut's emphasis on empathic immersion from the tradition of self-psychology (Kohut, 1984) both underline how essential it is for the therapist to be able to enter into the subjective world of the client in a concerned and empathic manner. This is very much part of any relational way of working to create for a client a sense of being understood by the therapist.

In addition to this, the emphasis in relational work is very much focused on the power of the counter-transference as a therapeutic resource. We refer readers to Karen Maroda's excellent book on this subject: *The Power of the Countertransference* (1991) in which she makes an eloquent case for the carefully considered use of the self-disclosure of counter-transference responses in therapy, particularly when the work appears to have reached an impasse. A relational therapist faces the challenge of bringing herself fully into the room and dealing directly with the relational impasses that occur between her and the client. This calls for the ongoing monitoring of our responses in relation to the unfolding process and a decision about what is useful to share in the interests' of the client's healing. There are no easy rules in this regard, a point Maroda makes so well; it depends more on the ongoing awareness on the part of the therapist of his own counter-transference and what he may learn from this, combined with a careful and respectful attention to the client's responses to the therapy. At times, the therapist may use his counter-transference awareness indirectly to understand the client's struggle more clearly, and at times the therapist may choose self-disclosure as a more powerful and appropriate option. What all these relational approaches share, however, is attention to the therapist's process in the therapy room as a valuable resource in the therapeutic process.

The therapeutic relationship is mutual but not symmetrical

A mutually constructed therapeutic relationship does not necessarily imply equality of influence or similarity of contribution. 'Mutual influence does not imply equal influence, and the analytic relationship may be mutual without being symmetrical' (Aron, 1991, p. 248). Mutuality does not imply an abrogation of the therapeutic role or task on the part of the therapist, rather it is an acknowledgement that two people cannot be in an encounter with one another without impacting on, or being impacted by, the other. Maroda (1991) speaks eloquently of the problem faced by therapists who are envious of their clients' success but will 'deny any wish to keep the patient down or to keep a patient dependent' (Maroda, 1991, p. 161); yet may unconsciously create a stalemate in the process of therapy. She encourages therapists to own their own envy and accept the inevitable 'de-idealization of the therapist' which characterizes the termination phase of the treatment (Maroda, 1991, p. 162). She speaks here of the possible emergence of 'countertransference dominance' a situation in which the 'treatment is dominated not by the patient's attempts to repeat the past, but by the analyst's' (Maroda, 1991, p. 49). She points out that the therapy may sometimes be dominated by the therapist's need to heal herself and the patient is vulnerable because the therapist has the authority to control the direction of treatment. What is called for here is courage and fortitude on the part of the therapist to explore and examine his own needs of the relationship so that these do not take the predominant place in the relationship and sabotage the process for the client.

An interplay between intrapsychic and interpersonal components in the process of therapy

Different approaches to psychotherapy differ in the degree to which therapy is regarded as a mutual relational process of healing *and* the extent to which it is viewed more exclusively as an opportunity for the client to gain insight into her own internal world, to understand his maladaptive patterns, to challenge her negative thoughts or to change his behaviours with the aid of the therapist as director. We consider that interplay between the client's internal world and the relationship between the client and others, in particular the therapist when he is in the therapeutic context, is inseparable. In the process of the therapeutic dialogue, a balance will need to be kept between a focus on the interaction between therapist and client and a focus on the client's internal world, 'between internal object relations and external object relations' (Aron, 1999, p. 253).

Hycner and Jacobs (1995) also speaks of the tension between the 'dialectical-intrapsychic' and the 'dialogical-interpersonal' aspects of the therapeutic endeavour. The 'dialectical-intrapsychic' as we understand this process refers to the client's internal dialogue between parts of the self and the relationship between self-as-subject and self-as-object described earlier. The 'dialogical-interpersonal' then refers to the client's

interaction with the therapist and others in their lives. As therapists we need to be attentive both to the inner conflicts of our
clients and to the relationship between the two of us in the
therapy room and between our clients and other people in
their world. Hycner believes that these two processes must be
attended to concurrently and that 'it requires considerable,
even masterful, attunement on the part of the therapist to
differentiate which needs to be emphasized at any moment
within the therapy' (Hycner and Jacobs, 1995, p. 74). We certainly view the process of therapy as a delicate movement
between focusing on the intrapsychic process of the client and
the exploration of the therapeutic relationship between us and
the client, as it unfolds in the therapy room. The client will
bring her past into the room with the therapist and create the
relationship in terms of her expectations of self, others and the
world. This material can be most effectively worked upon in
the here-and-now context of the therapeutic relationship.

The concept of 'inclusion' or the 'third-person perspective'

Such a relational approach aims at a place where client and
therapist alike can recognize the other as a separate person in
his/her own right whilst remaining in relationship with the
other. We see this as close to Buber's concept of inclusion
(Buber, 1923). Inclusion refers to a developing process where
a person is able to stay in his own world of experience,
empathize with the world of the other, and hold a metaperspective on this relational mutuality. Yontef (2002) whilst
writing of relational gestalt therapy considers 'inclusion' and
'confirmation' as the essence of true dialogue. He defines
inclusion as the capacity to put 'oneself into the experience of
the patient as much as possible, feeling it as if in one's own
body – without losing a separate sense of self. This confirms
the patient's existence and potential' (Yontef, 2000, p. 24).
This process of including the client and confirming the person's existence often provides the client with a reparative experience of relationship in the present. Yontef also stresses the
importance of the 'presence' of the therapist, 'being present as

a person meeting the person of the other' (op. cit., p. 24). This focus on the immediacy of meeting the other in the present moment is at the heart of authentic encounter. Such authentic meeting provides the other with an experience of being seen and acknowledged which may have been largely absent in their prior experience. Yontef (2002) makes the point that in this approach the therapist will also change as he feels a range of emotions in response to the client and is impacted by the experience of the other. This is at the heart of the concept of co-creation in relationship, this sense of mutual influence, of both persons changing in response to the other.

Aron (1999) too points out how the child gradually comes to experience the mother 'as a separate subject' in a movement from I–It relating to experiencing her as an 'I' in her own right (Aron, 1999, p. 246). We see this as similar to the progression in psychotherapy as the client first relates in an I–It manner to the therapist in line with Winnicott's idea of object usage (Winnicott, 1968) and then gradually begins to experience the therapist as a separate person, as an 'I' in her own right. We agree with Aron that this is at the heart of intersubjectivity which 'refers to the developmentally achieved capacity to recognize another person as a separate centre of experience' (Aron, 1999, p. 246). This is akin to Buber's notion of inclusion and is at the heart of mutuality in relationship.

We are reminded here too of the concept of reflective function which Fonaghy *et al.* (2002) regard as a developmental milestone for the growing child. Fonaghy *et al.* (2002) speak of 'mentalized affectivity' a term 'intended to indicate the capacity to connect to the meaning of one's emotions' so that one can be in tune with bodily experience and gain an experiential understanding of one's feelings (2002, p. 15). Mentalization or the reflective function refers to 'the development of the capacity to envision mental states in oneself and others' (Fonaghy *et al.*, 2002, p. 23) and in our view underlies the capacity for inclusion. The capacity for mentalization enables self-organization and affect regulation, capacities which underpin effective functioning. In realizing that the other is an 'I' who is separate, the child is developing a theory of mind: which is 'the developmental acquisition that permits children to respond not only to another person's behavior, but to develop a conception of the other's "beliefs, feelings, attitudes, desires, hopes, knowledge, imagination, pretense, deceit, intentions, plans and so on" ' (Fonaghy *et al.*, 2002, p. 35). This is the process by which children make their own and others' behaviour meaningful and informs all relationship building. This reflective function has both an interpersonal and a self-reflective aspect. In the process of psychotherapy, the therapist can focus on any of the three aspects of mentalized functioning: 'identifying, modulating, and expressing affects' (Fonaghy *et al.*, 2002, p. 437). These three processes are really a sequence, since we first need to identify affects before modulating them. We need to know what we feel before we can change the level of modulation or express affects (inwardly or outwardly) in a manner appropriate to the occasion. Also, expressing affect is dependent on the first two stages. This process as outlined by Fonaghy *et al.* (op. cit.) is reminiscent of the process of the gestalt cycle of experience where sensation is seen to precede awareness and the first two stages need to be addressed before the person can mobilize appropriate action and make good contact, a process that is well outlined by Clarkson (1989). What Fonaghy *et al.* (2002) contribute to the discussion is a detailed understanding of affect regulation and the modulation of affect in relation to the development of a person's reflective function.

Psychotherapy: an intersubjective relationship

Stolorow and Atwood (1992, p. 3) in describing the intersubjective nature of all relatedness stress how each party to the encounter bring their own inner experience to the meeting in a continual flow 'of reciprocal mutual influence'. They make clear that their use of the term 'intersubjective' may differ from the way in which it is used by developmental psychologists; they use it to refer to 'any psychological field formed by interacting worlds of experience, at whatever developmental level these worlds may be organized' (op. cit., p. 3). This is the sense in which we would use this term when talking of the co-creation of the therapeutic relationship. The therapist and client bring to their meeting the sum total of their experience to date in the ever-evolving process of human meeting. The consequence of this is that we too accept Stolorow and Atwood's view of transference and counter-transference as 'an intersubjective process reflecting the interaction between differently organized subjective worlds' of the therapist and client (op. cit., p. 2). In a co-creational view of relation, each partner is constantly contributing to the relationship whether she acknowledges this or not. There is no neutral interaction and the flow between the two people is changing the nature of the relationship in a process of ongoing mutual influence.

As therapists we bring to the therapeutic relationship our own contact styles and ways of constructing meaning from experience which then interact with those of the client. Bollas' concept of the 'unthought known' (Bollas, 1991) seems to us of relevance here, since there will be areas of experience for which the client has never found words and in the process of psychotherapy, the therapist will assist the client in a sensitive process of finding and putting words to hitherto 'unworded' experiences that have been 'known' only in a felt or bodily sense. Bollas (1991) sees 'the true self as the core of the unthought known' which is related to the 'inherited disposition that constitutes the core of personality' (Bollas, 1991, p. 279). However, it may be stating the obvious, but it is as well to stress that there will be areas of the therapist's experience that also fall into the realm of the 'unthought known', areas that he/she has never found language for and which will then remain outside of the 'spoken' arena of the therapeutic discourse, but may well exert a subtle influence on what the client experiences as taboo areas in the therapy. This is where supervision can play such a vital role since the supervisor may well draw the therapist's attention to such areas and invoke a discussion about these, leading to greater awareness of the processes at work in the therapy room.

It is this assumption that underlies our relational model of psychotherapy; that both therapist and client bring to the encounter the sum total of who they are in all their complexity with their own individual histories and ways of organizing their experience, their unconscious processes and the bodily expression of their areas of the 'unthought known' and are then faced with the challenge of meeting the other in all his/her complexity. It is, of course, the therapist's responsibility to build a bridge to the client, to use her awareness, skills, knowledge and experience to reach across the divide into the subjective world of the client. However, whether consciously or unconsciously, the client's experience will impact on the therapist, perhaps in images or dreams or affective responses, if not in words or ideas.

Similarly, the client will be responding on multiple levels to her experience of the therapist and registering the impact of the therapist on her whole being. The client may well pick up some aspect of the therapist's experience that the therapist may be unaware of: 'When for instance patients say that they think that I am angry at them or jealous of them or acting seductively towards them, I ask them to describe whatever it is that they have noticed that led them to this belief. I find that it is critical for me to ask the question with the genuine belief that I may find out something about myself that I did not previously recognize' (Aron, 1991, p. 252).

The manner in which the therapist interacts with the client will in some measure be influenced by the therapist's particular training background; gestalt therapists may use self-disclosure more readily than analytic or even person-centred therapists, but as soon as you accept a co-creational view of therapy, then questions of self-disclosure and therapist self-revelation in the room with the client form an unavoidable part of the discourse. 'Self-revelation is not an option; it is an inevitability' (Aron, 1999, p. 255). It is how explicitly we use our own experience and discuss this with clients that probably divides people from different orientations! This is perhaps most noticeable in the contrast between gestalt and psychoanalytic practitioners.

The six dimensions of the self which we described earlier will all be in the room and form part of the therapeutic discourse. At any moment we see that one dimension may be figural whilst the others are in the background depending on the particular preoccupations of the client. Following Kohut (1984) we think of the client as presenting different self–object needs at different times in the therapy and these will be related to the different dimensions of the self. The therapist will focus with the client on the particular dimension of self that is foreground and explore the client's experience of this self-experience.

Co-regulation of affect

Beebe and Lachmann (1998) referring to Fogel's work, speak of affect regulation as co-regulation, which fits well with our therapeutic task. 'It is a model of continuous, reciprocally evoked mutual regulation, where communication does not reside in either partner, but is continuously constructed by both' (op. cit., p. 484). We see this as the end goal of therapy, but do consider that at first the therapist will need to take greater responsibility for raising the person's awareness and working towards a state of mutual regulation as described earlier. Interestingly enough research suggests that the best predictor of secure attachment is 'midrange interactive coordination'; excessive self-regulation at the expense of interactive regulation leads to withdrawal; whereas over-vigilance is characterized by excessive monitoring of the partner at the expense of self-regulation (op. cit.). The aim is to achieve a balance between being aware of self and attending to the other, which feels very much in line with Buber's concept of inclusion (Buber, 1923, 1996) and for us forms the goal of a relational approach to psychotherapy.

Beebe and Lachmann (1998) stress that co-constructed regulation 'does not imply symmetry: each partner may influence the other in different ways, to unequal degrees' (op. cit., p. 485). In therapy this may well mean that at times the therapist may moderate their own contact style to help the client regulate affect up or down or make therapeutic choices to intervene in particular ways in the three-stage process described by Fonaghy and his associates. After all, the client is coming to the therapist so that he/she can benefit from the expertise of the professional. It is the task of the therapist to be aware of the client's process of affect regulation and the nature of the dysregulation and grade his/her therapeutic interventions accordingly. In this sense it behoves us as therapists to be sensitive to the client's relational rhythms and frame our interventions carefully in response to these established patterns of interaction.

We see the therapeutic relationship as moving along different stages from an It–It to an I–Thou relationship. In the previous discussion, we have indicated some of the processes involved in this evolution. In Part 3 these stages will be outlined and discussed in detail as we track the process of psychotherapy.

Locating our model and a critique of the model

Many commentators have claimed, in our opinion appropriately, that there has been an overemphasis in classical psychoanalysis and early-object-relations theory on a person's intrapsychic history and internal dynamics. This has often been described as a 'one-person psychology' or the 'myth of the isolated mind' (Stolorow and Atwood, 1992). However, we acknowledge that object-relations theory has the potential for a dialogical perspective to the extent that it recognizes a person as 'object seeking', with an innate tendency to seek relatedness with another. Winnicott in particular has emphasized how it is never possible to think of a person separately, since from birth onwards we are always in relation to the other.

Kohut's emphasis on the use of the other as self–object also focuses on an interpersonal dimension in the therapeutic relationship. However, the emphasis in self-psychology is very much on the provision of an empathic relationship by the therapist so that the client is able to use him in this 'self–object' manner to heal past deficits. In an essential sense, this is still 'a one-person' psychology as the therapist is not seen as an equal participant in the relationship, but is there to provide empathy for the person's self–object needs and understanding when there are misattunements. Following Kohut however, others such as Brandchaft, Stolorow and Atwood have focused on the interpersonal dimension in psychotherapy, in a branch of relational psychotherapy that they have named intersubjectivity theory. They state that from their perspective 'clinical phenomena ... cannot be understood apart from the intersubjective contexts in which they take form. Patient and analyst together form an indissoluble psychological system' (Atwoot and Storolow, 1984, p. 64). Intersubjectivity theory is committed to vewing the therapeutic relationship as an interactive, reciprocal process.

However, intersubjectivity theory is oriented mainly to the subjectivity of the client or the subjectivity of the therapist and, arguably, does not go as far as gestalt dialogical psychotherapy (Hycner, 1991) or relational psychoanalysis (Mitchell and Aron, 1999) in focusing on the relational ground between the participants, although it is focused on reciprocity of influence. In intersubjectivity theory as in other branches of self-psychology, clinical emphasis is on the therapist's stance of empathic attunement towards the client. In our view dialogical psychotherapy and relational psychoanalysis both extend the interhuman beyond that of intersubjectivity theory and push further the understanding of the richness of the relational nature of persons through their focus on the 'between' (dialogical therapy), or the 'relational unconscious' (relational psychoanalysis). The current focus in relational psychoanalysis stresses the co-construction of the therapeutic relationship and the importance of the analyst's subjectivity as part of this relational matrix (Aron, 1991). This is akin to the stance taken by gestalt dialogical therapists.

We see ourselves as drawing from both these rich traditions, from dialogical therapy within the humanist tradition (with its roots in existentialist thinking) and from relational psycho-analysis (and its allied branches such as intersubjectivity theory) within the psychoanalytic tradition. These relational approaches to psychotherapy currently share an emphasis on the importance of viewing the therapeutic relationship as a co-creation to which both participants contribute from their own subjective experience, consciously and unconsciously.

Nevertheless, in our opinion, all these relational approaches focus too heavily on the client-therapist dyad as an 'indissoluble psychological system' (Atwood and Stolorow, 1984). The 'within' or 'between' while absolutely essential to an under-standing of the client cannot in themselves address adequately the reality of people's daily lives. What goes on 'outside' (culture and ecology) and 'beyond' (the transpersonal) are further dimensions of human experience that need to be brought into the therapeutic endeavour. We consider these 'external' influences as a large part of what is also impacting on the client in the process of change.

In developing our view of the psychotherapeutic process, we have nevertheless been impressed by the similarity of ideas that are being articulated by contemporary self-psychologists like

Stolorow and Atwood (1984); by relational psychoanalysts like Mitchell and Aron (1999); by gestalt dialogic therapists like Yontef (2002); Hycner and Jacobs (1995); and by transactional analysts who espouse a relational perspective like Erskine and Trautmann (1996) and Hargaden and Sills (2002). There appears to be some convergence of ideas amongst these approaches even if the rapprochement amongst practitioners in the 'world out there' is slower to evolve. There is a growing emphasis in the therapeutic literature on the centrality of the therapeutic relationship as the vehicle of cure and on the importance of a two-person perspective on the psychotherapeutic process. Much of the impetus has come from contemporary research into child development supported by neurobiological findings that confirm the mutually interactive nature of the attachment process.

Critique of the model

We have endeavoured to place our model at this interface. We are the first to acknowledge that this is an ambitious project as we have endeavoured to draw together threads from widely divergent models. In taking such a wide view, we could well be seen as having spread our net too widely. However, we do see a convergence in the field of psychotherapy in the evolution of relational models in psychoanalysis and humanistic therapy that begin to resemble one another in certain essential assumptions especially in their emphasis on mutual co-creation, a focus on the process in the therapy room between the two participants as the main focus of the work, reciprocal influence in the therapeutic encounter and the use of the therapist's counter-transference as an essential therapeutic tool.

We acknowledge that in the area of techniques and strategies, we have raised a challenge, since relational therapists, while keeping their primary focus on 'what is happening in the room' will also draw on techniques from other approaches when these are helpful in the therapeutic endeavour. We see this as part of a general trend to put the client's needs, personality style, particular relational patterns, and unique history, into the frame as part of a mutual interacting process. It is then the responsibility of the therapist to modulate her own stance so that she can assist the client in a process of affect regulation: 'For example, for clients neglected by distracted, depressed parents, a spontaneous, interested, talkative way of being might be very important. On the other hand, a client with intrusive, demanding parents, and older siblings might find a silent, nonintrusive presence just what she needs for long stretches of time' (De Young, 2003, p. 37). This focus on the need for adaptability and versatility on the part of the therapist is at the heart of effective relational therapy, in our view, but it does mean that there is no easy rule book of techniques laid down for a particular client problem or presentation. It calls for a sensitive, relationally tuned attitude on the part of the therapist and an ongoing awareness of his counter-transference responses as a valuable source of information. We acknowledge that we are historically part of an exciting development in the broader field of relational psychotherapies across humanistic and psychoanalytic traditions and we are the first to see that we will inevitably be limited by our own place in this history.

In action, in the therapy room there will be differences (and similarities) in practice and we welcome both the similarities and the diversity as a rich potential source of learning for all of us. In the process of developing their own integrative frameworks, we encourage therapists to draw on contemporary research, inter alia, into areas such as psychotherapy outcome research, research into child and adult development and currently also into neurobiology to support their integrative frameworks as well as on the richness of clinical experience that is embedded in the theories and their applications that we have drawn upon in our discussions.

Part 3

Clinical case study – the practical application of theory

6 Assessment and diagnosis – 'It–It' relationship

Phillip is 48 years and until six months ago was the Accounts Manager for a medium-sized engineering company until being made redundant. The Human Resources Manager at Phillip's former employment suggested several weeks ago that Phillip contact me, though Phillip did not say why? His former company will fund four sessions of therapy as part of the redundancy package but Phillip did not indicate whether he anticipated any further therapy. Phillip appeared uncomfortable and irritated about coming to see me and expressed doubt about the value of our meeting since, he said, he was 'perfectly capable of sorting himself out' and finding alternative employment. The issue of alternative employment appeared Phillip's major concern.

Phillip has been married to Evelyn for 26 years and has two children, Patricia 24 years and Mark 22 years. Phillip has an older sister Francis 52 years with whom he has little contact, 'We have nothing in common and she has been spoilt by our mother all her life.' He also has a younger brother Anthony 44 years who he describes as a 'layabout'. Apparently he has been a 'roadie' for several music bands and is currently a DJ in nightclubs in the north of England. Phillip said 'it's high time Anthony grew up and assumed some responsibility'. He also expressed concern that his son, Mark, is 'taking after his uncle'. Mark dropped out of university in his final year and has had a series of casual jobs for the last 2 years. Currently Mark lives at home though Phillip thinks he should 'find a bed sit and stand on his own two feet'. Phillip and Mark argue a lot and this is a source of conflict between Phillip and Evelyn.

Evelyn trained as a primary school teacher but only taught for two years prior to the birth of her children. Since then she has not worked outside the home but helps out at a local charity 'hospice' shop and is secretary of the local church of England parochial council.

Phillip spoke more positively about his daughter Patricia who is 'store manager at a large regional supermarket and the youngest person to ever hold such a senior management position'. However, he expressed concern that the supermarket chain were exploiting her by requiring she work long hours and he somewhat cynically remarked that 'at the end of the day they (employers) don't give a damn as long as the accounts show a profit'.

Phillip has no significant medical history and has enjoyed good health most of his life playing squash on a regular basis at a sports facility owned by his former employer. He said he has not played for several weeks because he is feeling tired quite a bit and suffering some discomfort in his stomach. 'In any case', he said, 'my squash partners are still working for the company and I get bored listening to them going on about work all the time'. He spoke about this with aggression in his voice and tension in his body though he appears not to be aware of his body experience. He said his doctor also recommended that he follow up the advice of the Human Resource Manager and come to see me. Again Phillip did not say why his doctor made the recommendation.

Phillip looks young for his age with dark brown hair slightly greying at the temples. He has the athletic build of a man who has kept fit and active. At university, where he studied business administration, he had played rugby during the first two years of the degree course and also said he had explored Christianity and in recent years 'dabbled' in Buddhism. I was surprised because at first meeting Phillip does not impress as someone open to spiritual experience? In this context he went on to remark with an indifferent tone of voice, 'anyway the demands of work have left little time for playing around'. He also informed me, again as an aside, that at university he had been keen on photography, mostly landscapes and seascapes, but had let this drop as 'he never seemed to have the time'. In offering me this information about his spiritual interest and more artistic pursuits, albeit in an apparent throw away fashion, I intuited Phillip was showing me a softer side to him, searching for my reaction, but in a cleverly disguised way?

My initial impression of Phillip was of a man who had pursued a conventional and somewhat narrow path in life, until redundancy had shattered his carefully constructed world. He was clearly very angry and I imagined also scared, but he appeared unaware of this and out of touch with his feelings.

Phillip spoke of his family in a detached manner continuing to convey, at a superficial level, the apparent 'couldn't care less' attitude. In this first session it was very apparent that Phillip was 'not used to receiving help' but 'sorting things out on his own'. In this context he spoke briefly but significantly of his early life, describing his father as a self-made man, strict and opinionated. From quite poor and humble beginnings his father, Arthur, had built up a successful small building company and recently at the age of 76 he had handed over the directorship to a younger colleague but remained chairman of the Board. 'He'll die with his boots on', Phillip remarked with what appeared a mixture of pride and resentment. Apparently Arthur had encouraged his children to get a good education but then criticized university graduates as 'intellectuals' with no experience and little common sense. With such contradictory messages I imagine Phillip finds it hard to 'get it right' for his father and I intuited some deep hurt in his relationship with Arthur. I enquired of Phillip what his father's reaction had been to his redundancy and he replied in a detached manner 'Oh he just shrugged his shoulders and told me to "get on my bike" and find a better job.'

I further enquired 'Was that it'?

Phillip looked momentarily puzzled and replied with a hint of resentment 'Oh he was on his way to the golf club, nothing gets in the way of his precious golf.'

Phillip spoke disparagingly of his mother as 'a fussy and overly sentimental woman' who reads 'Mills and Boon' and visits the hairdresser for a weekly 'wash and set'. She takes pride in keeping the home clean and tidy and is devoted to Arthur. She does voluntary work with the Red Cross and helps out at a charity shop. Phillip seemed to despise his mother, but I also intuited a sense of longing or yearning, perhaps to penetrate her sentimentality and be touched by her at level deeper?

Phillip was less guarded in expressing his resentment towards his older sister who, it seems, is doted on by his mother.

He shared a certain sympathy for his sister's husband Derek, a local government housing officer who, according to Phillip is 'henpecked' by Francis and regularly humiliated by Arthur as a 'pen pusher who needs to get a proper job'.

In seeing his life as solely dominated by the problem of securing employment, and in his somewhat aloof and detached manner of speaking Phillip tends to objectify himself. He also objectifies the therapist by seeing me as someone expected to simply assist him to resolve the employment issue, though his professed ability to 'sort things out himself' tends to preclude collaboration. This 'It–It form of relating – objectifying self and other – is typical of the early stages of therapy when a client rarely has the self support or ego strength to be present with the whole of themselves – thoughts, feelings, physical experience, hopes and dreams.

This presentation may also reflect the initially strange, but arguably longed for, experience of most new clients of being alone with another person (the therapist) and being the primary focus of attention. Issues of safety and trust will be a major consideration for the client. Who is this person called a therapist? What is required of me? What can I expect from her/him? How much should I say? How much am I expected to say? What is allowed and not allowed? If I really say what I think and feel will I be judged? What are the rules in this new and unusual context of therapy? The client brings to the initial stage of therapy all the customs and expectations of conventional ways of relating which present a challenge to building the therapeutic alliance.

Reflecting on my initial counter-transference reaction to Phillip I am aware of a polarity in my emotional experiences towards him. On the one hand I feel angry in response to his arrogant and critical judgement of his sister, brother and son and fantasize a desire to 'cut him down to size'! As the session proceeds, however, I begin to feel increasing warmth towards Phillip's bewildered and vulnerable side and experience a sense of indignation at the injustice of his redundancy together with a desire to protect and console him. The former counter-transference reaction would reflect the repetitive dimension of the transference, inviting a repeat of the father–son relationship, 'get on your bike'. The latter counter-transference reaction would reflect the self–object dimension of the transference indicating unmet developmental needs and Phillip's longing for contact, specifically the need for mirroring – to be seen, heard and understood.

Two-thirds into this initial session I become aware that I am curious we have not yet made an initial contract about the length of therapy. We have discussed and agreed all other aspects of the business contract. Phillip has maintained, rather unconvincingly, his reason for coming to see me is to do with the issue of employment and has somewhat grudgingly shared something of his family background. However, I am intrigued that neither he nor I have yet discussed the duration of therapy?

I also begin to experience a dilemma because while at a conscious level employment appears Phillip's sole focus of interest, my counter-transference reaction towards him is intuiting a desire for a deeper level of communication than his surface presentation suggests. However, he is clearly avoiding any reference to what happens after the initial four sessions, paid for by his former employer.

So do we discuss a contract for the short term with a specific focus on the issue of employment or do we consider a longer contract to explore underlying issues that are already becoming apparent? For while the issue of the duration of therapy so far appears ambiguous Phillip has indicated, albeit in a heavily disguised fashion, significant underlying issues to do with his family of origin and his immediate family. I intuit that were I only to respond to his surface communication regarding the employment issue he may feel missed and not return to therapy, cynically consoling himself with the belief that he can sort this out for himself anyway. However, I also intuit that an invitation to consider a longer term contract might also be met with resistance from the introjected messages that demand he 'go it alone'. Consequently he may feel too threatened to continue with therapy?

An alternative possibility would be to suspend discussion of the duration of therapy and respond to my counter-transference by inviting the deeper level of communication Phillip appears to be unconsciously seeking? This clearly runs the risk of going too far too soon and engaging Phillip's defences against further therapy? However, Phillip's discomfort and barely concealed embarrassment at coming to see me at all render the prospect of his continuing in therapy very unlikely. I strongly suspect that unless we can establish some deeper level of contact today that will provide hope sufficient to overcome his acute embarrassment, then he will not return for a second session. So even though the therapeutic alliance is fragile and tentative I nevertheless decide to trust the unconscious invitation to contact that I intuit is coming from Phillip and take a risk. All the options are problematic and there appears nothing to lose as I invite Phillip to a deeper exploration of his issues. I do so by pointing out the incongruity between his somewhat cynical remarks and expressions of autonomy, and his apparent sad demeanour.

'Phillip, I experience you talking to me in an apparently unconcerned and indifferent manner, but at the same time you look very sad, is that right?'

Phillip looks surprised, alarmed even, and tears up. Choking on his words he apologizes while attempting to sound unaffected, 'Sorry, I didn't realise I was appearing so emotional.'

Phillip's resistance to his feelings touches me and I remark that it must be difficult to be in contact with his feelings and at the same time try and hold everything together?

Phillip replies, tearfully attempting and failing to appear unaffected, 'Sorry I am not used to showing myself like this, I'm ... sorry ... I'll be ok in a minute.'

I reply as a challenge to obvious introjects, 'Why do you think you have to apologise?' 'Isn't it ok to feel what you feel, Phillip?'

Phillip looks at me with what appears a range of conflicting emotions, anger, bewilderment, vulnerability and hope, and remarks rather confusedly, 'Not in my family ... a man doesn't show his feelings ... It's not ok ... is it'?

This latter remark appears both a statement and a question!

Phillip continues somewhat less defensively, 'Evelyn and I used to talk when we first got married but well ... work and kids and bills, you know how it is? But we haven't really talked about anything that matters for years.' Silently a single tear rolls slowly down his face and momentarily he stares at me very intently and I experience being scrutinised, but then he looks away and deflects his sadness with an angry remark, 'I don't think I would want to go back to my job anyway but I can't understand why they got rid of me? I have so much experience I just don't get it? It doesn't make sense and the new accounts manager is someone I trained. She is much younger than me so I guess it's about age, but Christ 48 isn't old, is it'?

As the session draws to a close Phillip looks uncomfortable and embarrassed. I imagine his self-exposure has left him anxious and he retreats to his earlier cynical presentation. I invite him to return next week at the same time and on the same day and he mutters a resentful goodbye and leaves abruptly.

In our experience change takes place in the space just beyond one's current optimum level of self-support, when we are pulled and challenged beyond what is comfortable and predictable. Phillip appears angry with me and I am left wondering whether he has exposed too much too soon and if he will return for the second appointment? Has he been pulled too far beyond his current level of self-support?

Diagnosis

Historically, humanistic and integrative psychotherapy has been antithetical to diagnosis partly in reaction to the psychiatric 'medical model' with its modes of diagnosis and classification, which can tend to 'treat the label rather than the patient'. Gilles De Lise believes the tendency to reject the idea of diagnosis is because it has been seen to be 'dehumanising, anti-therapeutic and politically repressive' (De Lise, 1991, p. 42). However, he claims the same criticism can be made towards those who refuse to diagnose for it can be equally dehumanising and anti therapeutic to deny the existence of differences between people. Furthermore, it is ironic that while denying real distinctions between our clients it appears indispensable to distinguish between some 400 schools of psychotherapy!

However, we perceive that over the past 20 years humanistic and integrative psychotherapies' have begun to assimilate aspects of psychiatry, psychoanalysis and developmental psychology into their own theoretical frames and developed diagnostic skills and clinical criteria that maintain the integrity of their approach (Evans, 1994, 1999).

In attempting to understand another human being most psychotherapies rely on

observation – descriptive statements about what is being noticed in the here and now, including physical presentation, affect, etc.

content – what is being said

subjective experience – what the therapist experiences in relation to the client

hypothesis – what sense the therapist makes of the above in terms of their own distinct theoretical frame.

At one end of a continuum classical Gestalt psychotherapy adopts a phenomenological perspective with the emphasis on awareness at the contact boundary and with the focus on the observation of the here-and-now of experience. By attending to what is being noticed in the moment (phenomenological focusing) – how Phillip looks, speaks, breathes, hears, moves etc., an aspect of his behaviour will eventually become a focus of interest and a figure or pattern (gestalt) will emerge. This may lead to a diagnosis – 'Phillip seems to be deflecting from his feelings?' Traditionally Gestalt psychotherapy has been predominantly functionally oriented.

At the other end of the continuum classical psychoanalysis has tended to be aetiologically oriented, relying largely on the content of a client's verbal expression to focus on how past, the there-and-then, has shaped and determined the present, the here-and-now.

Our integrative approach is grounded in a wider perspective that includes the past, the present and the future. A focus that relied too heavily on Phillip's history would lose the immediacy of the present moment, including the significance of contextual influences from the environment. A focus which stays close only to Phillip's immediate experience would not allow for the continuity of his experience over time (Melnick and Nevis, 1992, p. 60). Our contact focus is therefore interested in the sum of the ongoing here-and-now experiences, that is, the therapeutic relationship. 'Everyone's life is worth a novel,' the past is relevant for it is the story of how Phillip arrived at the present (Polster, 1987). Finally, research has indicated

that hope in and for the future, including hope in the therapeutic endeavour, is an essential ingredient in psychotherapy
outcome. (Hubble *et al.*, 2000). Further important contributions to the significance of hope in psychotherapy include
Cooper (2000) and Yalom (1995).

Our integrative approach to diagnosis, described later, was
first presented at a European Gestalt conference in Paris in
1991 (Evans, 1994, p. 42) and has subsequently been further
developed. The model retains the phenomenological focus on
the here-and-now of Gestalt psychotherapy but includes the
relational and development foci by including critical reflection
on both the therapeutic relationship and the significance of
Phillip's past.

Gary Yontef (1988) 'classifies' the client's experience into
what he calls time zones:

The here-and-now – Phillip's whole self-environment field at
                    a particular moment
The there-and-now – Phillip's life outside therapy
The here-and-then – What happened in the therapy room a few
                    moments ago, last week, last month, last
                    year
The there-and-then – Phillip's history, the background from
                    which meaning emerges.

These four time zones together with their respective major
focus of interest may be included in our diagnostic model thus:

Time zone	Perspective	Focus of interest
Here-and-now and there-and-now	Functional	Functional and Dysfunctional behaviour
Here-and-then	Relational	Contact and resistance transference
There-and-then	Developmental	Repetition and self–object dimensions

Here-and-now and there-and-now

The first two time zones together provide information for a diagnosis of Phillip's observed functional and dysfunctional behaviour at the contact boundary, compatible with the phenomenological bias of many humanistic psychotherapies, especially Gestalt psychotherapy. In describing behaviour at the contact boundary we observe the way Phillip uses his contact functions, that is, how does he 'look, move, speak, breathe, touch, manifest that he has not achieved object constancy or has not a coherent sense of self?' (De Lise, 1991, p. 44). We include an analysis of Phillip's contact functions in detail in the Appendix.

This analysis suggests that Phillip interrupts contact with himself by not acknowledging or understanding the significance of his physical sensations and therefore being somewhat emotionally illiterate. Figure 6.1 illustrates how Phillip blocks contact with himself and others so that he rarely completes an experience to full satisfaction. Instead he tends to disengage with himself and others before the action phase of the cycle. Though he does appear to be a quite sensitive man it is difficult for him to identify what he is feeling. In contact with others he appears to have difficulty relating at an intimate level and presents himself as somewhat aggressive, though he appears not to be aware of this. Consequently he impresses as a somewhat lonely individual with few, if any close friends, but one or two former work colleagues whom he meets solely at a social level through playing squash, a very physical game which can be highly competitive.

From this analysis of his observed behaviour we can reflect with Phillip on the purpose of his dysfunctional behaviour and explore how it is maintained, that is, what specific defence mechanism or modes of resistance does he use to maintain his habitual patterns of thinking, feeling and behaviour? By engaging Phillip in collaboration with his own healing we can develop and strengthen the therapeutic alliance and help prepare the ground for a more thorough I–Thou engagement later in therapy.

Figure 6.2 illustrates how Phillip maintains these defences against self awareness and self in relation to others through retroflection, deflection and projection. By the process of

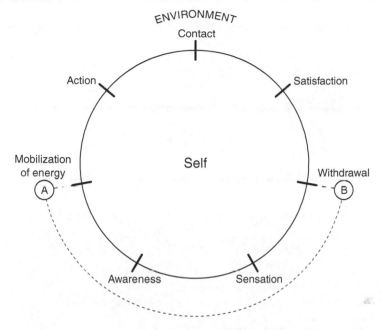

Phillip is blocking contact with himself and
the therapist at the initial phases of the
gestalt cycle A–B

Figure 6.1 Dysfunctional behaviour patterns
Source: Clarkson, P. (1989)

retroflection (Perls *et al.*, 1951/94) he turns emotions, like
anger, back in on himself with likely consequences for his
physical health. Through deflection (Polster and Polster,
1974) he avoids direct engagement with the therapist, others
and uncomfortable issues, especially the hurt he appears to
hold inside? Through projection (Perls *et al.*, 1951/94) he
disowns feelings and attributes them to others, especially
criticism.

We imagine all these defences are grounded in introjection
(Perls *et al.*, 1951/94). This is the process by which as a child,
Phillip would have 'swallowed whole' the 'rules', values, atti-
tudes and behaviours of his parents, usually reinforced by

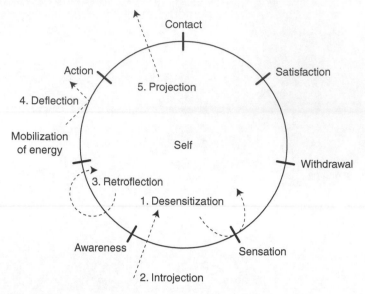

Figure 6.2 Maintenance of dysfunctional behaviour patterns

Notes

1. Phillip desensitizes his feelings.
2. Desensitization is supported by introjected messages about the 'inappropriate-ness' of emotional expression.
3. When Phillip's emotions are more than he can bear then he retroflects them, that is, holds them inside his body which becomes rigid with shallow breathing, clenched fists and tight jaw.
4. Phillip deflects from contact with the therapist.
5. Phillip projects criticism on to the therapist and further, defends against contact.

forms of punishment and sanctions. His sense of security and well being and, psychologically speaking his very survival in the world, would have depended on his primary caregivers. In order to survive Phillip, like all children, will have sacrificed himself – his needs, wants, desires and feelings, to greater or lesser degree, by adapting to the demands of his parents. This creative adjustment is the best he could have done to survive and is the basis of the introjection.

In Figure 6.3 we Illustrate, through a series of incomplete circles, how the child's creative adjustment is borne out of, and is a consequence of, numerous experiences of incomplete gestalten, that is, experiences in relation to self and others where the child's needs are deliberately or otherwise inter-rupted. While a child is invariably dogged and persistent in the pursuit of their needs there comes a point at which they will 'close down' on a need(s). Time and again in psychotherapy we encounter clients whose unmet developmental need(s) are primarily the result of parental neglect or abuse but who protect the parents, and hence themselves, by refusing to acknowledge parental responsibility. As a child they 'took responsibility' for the deficits in their environment. This 'creative adjustment' will have protected them against the reality of parental inade-quacy but at the cost of 'swallowing whole' some notion con-firming their own inadequacy, failure or 'badness'. Collectively the sum total of Phillip's numerous introjected messages constitute what has been called his 'life script' (Berne, 1961). We perceive the life script to be a person's basic intrapsychic process, that is, what they think about themselves, others and the world.

A person's intrapsychic structure will in turn influence the nature and quality of their interpersonal relationships and usu-ally in such ways as to reinforce, through the repetition com-pulsion, the life script (Berne, 1975). Together a person's life script and their pattern of interpersonal functioning will rein-force each other to maintain the status quo. This is the basis for resistance, which we understand to be the client's way of surviving in the here-and-now, including the here-and-now of the therapy session. Figure 6.3 also illustrates the possibility, via the self–object transference, of moving out of dysfunctional behaviour patterns and finding healthier ways of relating to self and others

The analysis of Phillip's contact functions provides helpful information about his personality which enables us to integrate a mental health classification into our diagnostic model. While a person may 'act out of character' in the moment nevertheless their behaviour is relatively stable over time so that we are able to attribute to them a more or less fixed identity. We 'know' how they (and us) are likely to behave in most situations so that a sense of predictability develops in our relations with self and others. De Lise defines personality specifically as the way a person organizes the cognitive, emotive and behavioural com-ponents of their experience, which gives a sense of identity.

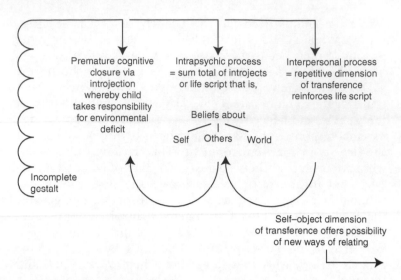

Figure 6.3 Creative adjustment

This sense of identity and how it impacts on others and the environment in general, is personality.

Personality is thus the relatively predictable ways in which a person functions at the contact boundary. De Lise connects this understanding of personality with the Diagnostic Statistical Manual of the American Psychological Association and in particular the section on personality disorders thus, 'personal pathology arises out of a meeting of the organism and the environment. The configuration of the field overwhelms the client's capacity to organise the field at the time. The client is not "sick" as such, but at the contact boundary something that may result in harmony and interconnectedness results in suffering.' The client's inability to manage the contact boundary so as to be nourished is the clinical syndrome – axis 1; the client's relatively stable and maladaptive performance at the contact boundary is the personality disorder – axis 2 (De Lise, 1991, p. 45).

In the DSM the criteria for diagnosing the dozen or so personality disorders are, for the most part, based on manifest descriptive 'pathology' rather than inferences or criteria from presumed causation. Thus the criteria are compatible with the phenomenological attitude. Furthermore, in order to accommodate the multiplicity of peoples' lives and experiences the

DSM uses a multi-axial system that reflects the systemic character of psychopathology so that '... the five axis of diagnosis are not simply additive and linear but constitute subsystems interacting dynamically with one another and is thus compatible with field theory' (De Lise, 1991, p. 44).

We replace the notion of personality disorder in the DSM with that of personality orientation which we further see as a continuum from mild to severe to chronic. This latter chronic presentation we would identify as a disorder of the personality. Of course most clients' presenting for psychotherapy do not have a personality disorder but by carefully integrating use of the DSM into our diagnostic model we have access to the clinical wisdom of psychiatry and psychology that provide further information to help make sense of our clients' overwhelming experiences.

Through an analysis of Phillip's contact functions, and by critical reflection of the relational and developmental components of our diagnostic model Phillip appears to have a surface presentation of Passive Aggressive. However, we suspect that this is a rather vulnerable and precarious means of defending himself in relationships against an underlying deep hurt that has led to a creative adjustment that appears a combination of the Avoidant and Narcissistic personality types.

His narcissism is not the flamboyant grandiose character represented in the DSM but several narcissistic characteristic behaviours are evident: self-sufficiency and a fear of reliance on others; fear of criticism and 'getting it wrong'; not being good enough and an enduring sense of shame about this. Such a person when getting one single criticism on a school report among other overwhelmingly positive feedback would not be able to delight in the positive, but likely dwell on the single negative comment. However, if he were to only receive positive feedback he would find the praise extremely uncomfortable, embarrassing and even experience shame, because his unconscious yearning and longing for praise would be revealed and his deep neediness exposed.

Phillip may have developed an avoidant front to conceal his narcissism? He appears to desperately want to succeed in order to feel good about himself, but he must not be seen to succeed! Being a child of the twentieth century, Phillip was brought up

in a nuclear family and clearly inculcated the values of autonomy and self sufficiency. Without the support of the extended
family of earlier generations he, like most of his generation,
would harbour a deep yearning, which leaves him afraid of 'being
seen' yet terrified of 'not being seen' (Epstein, M., 1996). In the
western world there appears to be a deficit of the mirroring
self–object transference. This appears a structural problem in
western society because it is part and parcel of the culture of
modern life.

Here-and-then

The therapeutic relationship provides a microcosm of Phillip's
way of being in the world but so much of what we need to
know, in order to describe and understand him, will simply not
be available at the outset of therapy, and will not always be
immediately observable in the here-and-now of the therapeutic encounter, but instead will only be revealed over time,
in the nature and quality of the contact between us, including
the transference and counter-transference. Referring to a transaction between us as transference does not, we maintain, mean
that Phillip's behaviour is distorted. On the contrary, we believe
the transference is a significant component of Phillip's phenomenological way of being in the world, his creative adjustment and way of making sense of the world, including the
world of the therapy room.

Therefore, it is essential to understand as much as possible
of Phillip's phenomenology throughout the course of therapy,
not simply at the beginning. To make an initial diagnose of
Phillip as a mix of passive aggression, avoidant and narcissistic
will be to 'label' him in a dehumanising way if we do not fill
in what this means in relation to Phillip's individual and specific ways of being at the contact boundary, which will be
played out over time in the therapeutic relationship.

Francis Allen (1987) describes how each of the different
personality types present fairly typical transferential organization which elicit typical counter-transference responses from
the therapist. The ongoing emotional response of the therapist
to the client is therefore additional diagnostic information that

helps confirm or challenge the initial diagnosis and thus connects the first three time zones. This means that the therapist's subjective experience becomes an important aspect of the diagnosis assessment, which in turn helps to bring to awareness the contribution that the therapist may be making to block the work (Keisler, 1996).

There-and-then

From our integrative perspective the past does not cause the present but out of the original infant-primary/care-giver field, patterns of relating are formed which tend to continue habitually and out of awareness throughout life, and especially in times of stress or crisis. These relational patterns emerge in the therapeutic relationship as resistance, often in the transference and counter-transference. However, these relational patterns were developed by the client primarily in order to survive and as such represent their 'creative adjustment' (Perls *et al.*, 1951/94). From this perspective resistance is a client's coping strategy and may be respected as the best solution they could find in the past, while working with the client to discover more fruitful ways of being in the present.

An understanding of developmental issues is essential in order to understand what is going on in the therapeutic relationship in all four time zones. Inter-subjectivity theory and Self-psychology, together with the work of Daniel Stern, provide perspectives on child development that we have found to be significant in our work with clients. These perspectives are compatible with the phenomenological, holistic and field theoretical bases of a range of humanistic and integrative therapies so that their integration into our approach to integrative psychotherapy can be made without compromise or loss of integrity (Tobin, 1990, pp. 14–63).

It is now possible to see how the above may be brought together to provide an integrative diagnosis. The initial observations and descriptions of Phillip's functional and dysfunctional behaviour at the contact boundary may be supported, or challenged and modified, by what emerges in the therapeutic relationship and especially in the transference. In turn what emerges in the transference will provide significant insights into his developmental history, and especially the ways in which his development needs have not been met. Developmental deficits will become apparent in the repetitive and self–object dimensions of the transference.

Thus for us there is no such thing as the past. There is history but the past is always present in the ground and may emerge as figural in the here-and-now. Especially in times of stress we notice that the past can become actively present while hitherto current foci of interest retire to the background. We find that assessment and diagnosis helpful in organising all the information coming to us from the client and from within the relationship between us, and allowing more consideration of various strategic interventions as well as supporting some degree of prediction in the unfolding of the therapy. We also find that assessment and diagnosis can be a grounding experience for us by acting as a kind of brake preventing us moving precipitously and instead facilitating critical reflection on the process of therapy (Melnick and Nevis, 1992).

If personal 'pathology', or as we prefer the phrase, creative adjustment, arises out of a meeting of the individual with the environment it is vitally important to take seriously toxicity in the environment at large. Psychotherapy has tended to towards a preoccupation with the individual but much of what we hear in the therapy room amounts to a social critique. Why is 48 years considered 'past it' in contemporary business culture? Why is experience considered less relevant, or even irrelevant in relation to youth? What are the implications for our clients, in terms of the quality of their relationships, of societal definitions of maturity as autonomy? To ignore cultural, political, economic, spiritual and green issues, we may be passively political and unwittingly facilitate the client to adapt to pathology in the environment. Might not this then render therapy part of the toxic environment itself and amount to professional pathology?

7 Intrapsychic focus – 'I–It' relationship

The following week Phillip does return to therapy but is five minutes late. His body is rigid and he appears tense. He sits down with arms folded across his chest and legs crossed, and staring at the wall directly behind me he makes a rather sullen and defiant apology blaming the traffic.

I feel irritated and dismissed by what I perceive as passive aggressive behaviour and I speculate he is inviting rejection.

In a rather forced innocuous tone of voice, and through clenched teeth Phillip remarks, 'We didn't sort anything out last week, about the work situation, you just asked questions about my past, how that's going to help?' I sense an invitation to justify myself and speculate that his critical father is present in the transference. I decide to reply with a paradoxical response, 'I don't know Phillip', which is both true and a challenge to that aspect of his script that requires him always to 'get things right'. I continue, 'I acknowledge your need to explore the work situation and I am also interested in you as a person.'

Phillip looks momentarily confused and a little disarmed and was clearly not expecting this response. He is silent for a moment or two and then replies with open hostility in his voice, 'Well what's the point? How is four weeks with you going to make any damn difference?'

My immediate reaction is a feeling of relief that the passive aggression has been replaced with a more direct expression of anger. I also realize that Phillip came last week with the assumption that we would only be meeting for four sessions? Given what we surmise about his history of poor mirroring from his parents I appreciate why he is angry. I further realize that in the first session the misunderstanding and lack of clarity around the contract may well have been a parallel process.

His history of 'being missed' repeating itself in the very first meeting.

I reply 'Phillip I appreciate your open expression of anger and the duration of therapy is negotiable. Perhaps it would have been helpful if I had clarified that with you last week?' Here I take responsibility for the confusion around the therapy contract, which may possibly be an unusual experience for Phillip in his relations with others, especially those in positions of authority?

He looks initially perplexed and is then quiet and thoughtful for some time. When he eventually speaks his manner is respectful and grows increasingly earnest. Making good eye contact with me he says, 'Look, to be frank the job situation is not really a problem just now. We are reasonably comfortable financially and ... well ... what I want is to be doing something ... well ... worthwhile you know?'

He scrutinizes my reaction and apparently reassured he continues, 'I don't know what that will be, but I don't want to return to the sort of work I have been doing all my life, it's a dead end. I feel I want to take some time to sort my life out and when I left last week I couldn't see how four weeks would do that. I guess because the old firm agreed to pay for four weeks that was it, that's how long I got.'

A number of factors have enabled Phillip to be more forthcoming: the knowledge that the duration of therapy is negotiable is clearly figural but several factors in the therapeutic relationship (currently the background to the therapy) are significant, though out of Phillip's awareness; the modelling by the therapist of 'not having to know', which, in view of his life script, we surmise would be permission giving; the non-judgmental acceptance of his open expression of anger which acknowledges or 'sees' a hitherto unacceptable side of himself; the therapist taking responsibility for the lack of clarity around the contract which will have given a different experience around the exercise of power?

'Phillip we can negotiate the duration of the therapy contract. Is there anything else you would like more clarity about regarding therapy?'

'Yeah (he shares an open and engaging smile quite distinct from my experience of him until now) What is therapy exactly,

I mean I have some idea but ...'? (Phillip's voice trails off and he looks at me expectantly).

We believe that an initial understanding of the purpose and nature of therapy is important in creating the therapeutic alliance and in keeping with the goal of I–Thou relating. As therapy continues so Phillip's understanding will deepen and grow. We suggest that an analogy in the form of a story may be a very useful way of presenting therapy because it can invoke a sense of hope and possibility, while at the same time conveying a flavour of the process of therapy – both the highs and lows. Furthermore, description in the form of a story also provides space for the client to invest their own meaning.

'Phillip, over the years I have found it useful to convey a flavour of the purpose and process of therapy in the form of a brief story. It is of a well-known historical event and I can't recall where I first read or heard of it in the context of therapy but you may find it helpful?'

Philip's cynicism has now receded to the background and he leans forward in his chair and looks engaged and interested.

'You will recall the story of Christopher Columbus who with a small flotilla of ships set out on a voyage of discovery?'

Phillip nods and leans forward some more.

'Well there were times during his adventures at sea when the wind blew strong and fair and the small ships made good progress. But there were times when the wind fell away completely, the sea turned to glass and the ships floated rudderless and seemingly endlessly, stuck in the doldrums for weeks on end. And there were times when the thunder roared and the lighting flashed, gale force winds brought relentless torrents of rain, and huge waves threatened to overwhelm the ships and crew. Well Phillip, the experience of therapy can reflect all three descriptions of this epic voyage.'

Phillip swallowed hard and looked curious. I paused for a moment or two and further added 'Columbus had set out to discover a new route to India but instead discovered a new world!'

After a while Phillip took a deep breath and said, with what I sensed was a measure of excitement 'So you don't know what's going to happen really?'

I reply 'Well normally you would set the agenda but where will it lead? That's open ended.'

Phillip continues, 'And I can talk about anything here?'

'Yes Phillip, nothing need be censored.'

Phillip is quiet for some time and then tells me in almost hushed tones 'My doctor told me he thought my insomnia and stomach pain were symptoms of depression ... what do you think?'

I sense embarrassment perhaps shame, 'You are telling me this in hushed tones. Is this a secret Phillip?'

Rather indignantly he replies 'well I don't want the world to know do I?'

'Is there anyone in particular that you would not want to know?'

Phillip is quiet for a while and then says 'Well really I don't want anyone to think I'm depressed ... my children ... Evelyn ... my father, yeah especially him.'

'How come?'

'Well I would feel I was letting my children down, setting a poor example I suppose.'

'And your father?'

'He would give me a hard time and make out I was weak and tell me to "get my act together", the ...' (mumbles incoherently).

'How would that make to feel, Phillip?'

'Pissed off actually ... he never does anything but criticize.'

I sense Phillip scrutinizing me closely again, I imagine to gauge my reaction to his overt expression of anger. Apparently reassured he continues for the remainder of the session to unload, in general terms, his anger towards his father but then deflecting his anger to his redundancy.

We end the session with establishing an open-ended contract in terms of the duration of therapy and with an expressed desire for greater self-understanding and new direction in life.

We believe that what has brought Phillip back to therapy and led to an open-ended contract regarding the duration of therapy, is the relational developmental aspect of therapy. Specifically, the mirroring self–object transference has been initiated and is being addressed by the therapist's I–Thou stance towards Phillip and by the containment provided by the non-judgmental attitude of therapy. We agree with Kohut that, out of their awareness, clients may attend therapy to address unmet developmental needs. Of course, at this stage Phillip is not conscious of this underlying process and unaware of his deep desire to be seen and met. He does not have the self support (ego strength) to allow this into awareness and will likely remain 'issue driven' for some time.

During this 'I–It' phase of therapy we support Phillip to develop his sense of entitlement which has been thwarted and blocked in its development. He requires permission to think his own thoughts, experience his own emotions, dream his own dreams. In a way we support Phillip to a necessary level of egotism in order to strengthen his sense of himself, his 'I'. So in this phase of therapy we focus on a range of clinical skills – techniques and strategies of intervention – to support and challenge Phillip to address his introjects and thereby challenge his life script. We do so respectfully recognising that life script is creative adjustment, Philip's way of surviving in the world.

At this early ego-building phase of therapy we understand the therapeutic relationship to be crucial to the therapeutic alliance but the relationship itself is not the focus of therapy and remains in the background. The focus of therapy is on the 'I' of the client and the therapist remains, in the awareness of the client, largely objectified. The relationship is, from the client's perspective, essentially 'I–It'. In the unconscious of the client of course a deeper alliance with the therapist is taking shape and is growing and developing and will emerge in the next phase of therapy as the major focus of the therapeutic endeavour when the focus becomes 'I–Thou', and techniques fade more into the background as contact becomes the major focus.

It is impossible to predict how long the 'I–It' phase of therapy will last, six months, one year, two years or more? However, an important indicator that the therapy is moving into the 'I–Thou' phase is somewhat obvious when the client focus begins to switch from issues to do with their life outside therapy, past and present, to issues emerging for the client within the therapeutic relationship. The therapist becomes more the focus of therapy and to a large extent much of the work done in the preceding phases is replayed at a deeper level in the 'I–Thou' phase. That is, the intrapsychic work addressed in the 'I–It' phase is replayed via the interpersonal and with greater intensity as developmental issues from the 'there-and-then', emerge in the transference in the 'here-and-now' and are played out again and worked through. In this mutually demanding phase of therapy the client moves back and forth between 'I–Thou' and 'I–It' relating. Eventually, and again with unpredictable time scale, a fairly constant and mutual 'I–Thou' relationship will be established and the issue of endings will begin to emerge as the prelude to the final end phase of therapy.

A crucial concern in all phases of therapy is that of client resistance. We agree with Arkowitz that there are different types of resistance that have different roots and need to be worked with differently (Arkowitz, 2002).

We also agree with Mahoney that an important component of resistance to change is anxiety and the desire for self protection (Mahoney, 1991). This is compatible with the gestalt view of resistance as creative adjustment – survival.

At different times throughout the course of therapy the therapist will need to reflect on the differing nature and presentation of client resistance. In this 'I–It' phase of therapy when the focus is on the intrapsychic world of the client, a different approach to working with resistance will be required than in the 'I–Thou' phase when the focus shifts more to the interpersonal relationship.

The 'I–It' phase of therapy with Phillip lasted some 14 months when together Phillip and I identified patterns of behaviour and explored his life script through focusing on specific introjects. Gradually he is able to identify ways in which he has maintained and reinforced self-defeating behaviours. In particular, Phillip becomes increasingly aware of his need to 'Be Strong' and hide his feelings, coupled with his fear of 'getting it wrong'.

A key episode in therapy occurred about 10 months into therapy when Phillip begins to recognize the impact of his 'Be Strong' introject on his capacity for intimacy and, in particular, his tendency to cynicism and sarcasm as a way of protecting himself. He came to therapy very distressed about a row with his son, Mark, and described his behaviour towards his son as 'over the top'. The incident took place over the preceding weekend when Mark was to meet with Phillip at a large DIY

Superstore, to help carry and load several packs of bricks, sand and cement to repair a section of the garden wall. Mark did not turn up and Phillip reluctantly phoned his father for assistance. His father was about to leave to play golf and refused to help so Phillip returned home empty handed and furious. Mark was still in bed and, according to Phillip, he 'lost it' with his son and an 'almighty row took place' during which he screamed highly offensive comments at his son 'You're a complete waste of space', 'A lazy good for nothing idiot', 'A fool who is going nowhere in life', 'A scrounger and a waster and I want you out of this house today.'

Mark screamed abuse back and finally accused him of being 'just like granddad'. This had infuriated Phillip even more and he was on the verge of hitting Mark when Evelyn intervened and with an uncharacteristically angry outburst exclaimed, 'It's true Phillip you behave just like your father and I'm completely fed up with it.' Phillip immediately left the house slamming the doors and breaking a pane of glass in the conservatory door. Over the past few days he has been unable to speak to Evelyn or his son, but has felt very guilty, embarrassed, upset and confused as to what to do or say?

Intensity of emotion together can often lead to a lack of clarity of thinking for client's, like Phillip, who strongly retroflect. A poor ability to deal with strong emotions overwhelms, to a greater or lesser extent, the ability to think and respond appropriately to self and others. This may be worked through in therapy by inviting the client to experiment (Zinker, 1978) by spontaneously addressing the relevant absent persons in the form of a cushion(s). In the safety of the therapeutic environment and with some distance between himself and the event Phillip can exercise less censorship than would be likely when speaking directly to the person(s). Catharsis may then, in turn, allow sufficient expression and discharge of feelings to enable greater clarity of thought and increased awareness. So I invite Phillip to choose two cushions in the room, one to represent his wife and the other his son, and say whatever he wants and, in order to generate immediacy, to do so in the first person present tense?

Philip agreed and having chosen two cushions and placing them side by side directly in front of him and some two meters away, he looked at them for a moment or two and began to cry. He sobbed deeply and wordlessly for a couple of minutes and then, taking a deep breath he said to them both, 'I'm so sorry, so very sorry.' He sobbed again for several minutes and then turned to me and said 'I need to talk to my father.'

I invited Phillip to choose a cushion to represent his father and he pointed to a large red cushion requesting that I place it at some distance away. I intuited he was anxious, perhaps frightened about simply touching the cushion and possibly somewhat regressed? In such circumstances it is important to honour the anxiety in the client and so I suggested a change in the experiment. Placing the cushion at some distance away I suggested he speak to me about his father and in the third person past tense. In this way the intensity and immediacy is reduced in order to diminish the degree of anxiety and enable completion of the experiment. Specifically the level of difficulty of an experiment needs to be gauged to the level of self-support of the client in order to deal with resistance.

Phillip appeared relieved at the suggested change to the experiment and began to speak to me about his father.

'Well he's always been very strict ... um ... (Phillip hesitates) ... He's achieved a lot in his life um ... um ... through hard work ...' (Phillip's energy is very low and there is little sense of conviction in his voice which is flat. He is not looking at the cushion or me, but talking to the ground in front of him.).

After a minute or so of silence Phillip looks at me directly and he appears a little dissociated, 'I need to talk to him but I can't seem to be able to?'

'Phillip do you mean that a part of you wants to speak to your father and another part of you does not?'

'Yes.'

'Well, I suggest we change the experiment and give you the opportunity to explore both parts separately. This can be done by a process called two chair work. I place two chairs in front of you and opposite each other. The one can represent that part of you that wants to speak to your father, while the other chair can represent that part of you that does not want to speak to your father. You can sit on either chair in turn but speak only from that position designated to a specific chair. You can start where you like. Do you want to engage in this experiment? Phillip agrees and first sits in the chair that wants to speak to his father, but after a moment or two switches to the chair that does not want to speak to his father, but then returns almost immediately to the first chair again.' Resistance to this technique is greater at its commencement but usually diminishes as the client proceeds and begins to engage.

Phillip speaks quietly and sadly, 'There's things I need to say ... things I never said ... (hesitates) ... I am 48 and still bloody scared to talk to him.' Phillip looks at me and getting up he says to me 'I think I need to be on this other chair' and swoops over.

'I'm scared of him. When I'm around him I feel small and I don't want to talk to him because I'm scared of him.' Phillip looks at me again and says 'No that's not right somehow', Phillip goes back to the chair that wants to speak to his father, 'I need to tell him so I can move on. Some how my father is influencing my life in ways that I don't want. I don't want to be like him. I'm scared of him'... silence for a minute or two when Phillip looks very thoughtful.

He switches chairs and from that part of him that doesn't want to speak he says clearly and with conviction to the large red cushion which I, accidentally (?) left in the same place when we changed the experiment 'I'm afraid to speak to you because I'll be angry with you and if I'm angry with you?'... hesitates and voice trembles as he says ...'if I'm fucking angry with you, you won't like me, you won't love me ...' Phillip begins to cry but his anger takes precedence and he says to me, 'I understand why a part of me doesn't want to speak to him, it's because I have been scared of him not loving me if I tell him I'm angry with him.' Phillip is quiet and thoughtful for some time and then declares ...'now I want to go back to the first thing (experiment) I did, I want to talk to that cushion over there, face that bastard head on, ok with you?'

I nod my support as he moves into position on the floor facing the red cushion some four meters away. Loudly and clearly and with strength and energy Phillip says, 'All my life and I've never heard you approve of anything I've done. When I got into university you took the piss out of "intellectuals", when I got a 2:1 you said "Is that the best you can do" meaning that's not good enough. When Evelyn and I bought our first house you found something to criticize about it, something about it being an unwise area to invest in. Well you were wrong weren't you? Not that you can ever admit to it, the area has been developed and new amenities built including the improvement of the park so it is an attractive area to live now and you're pissed because you didn't buy building land around here and missed out on turning a few quid profit.'

I notice Phillip is clenching his fists very tightly and out of awareness punching the arms of his chair. However, I am aware that the session is drawing to an end and decide not to direct Phillip's attention to this as it usually signals the commencement of experimentation with the physical expression of anger. Client safety, particularly the 10-mile drive to his home, indicates it is too close to the end of the session for him to engage in this way today. Instead I indicate the time to Phillip and suggest we finish the session by him consolidating his awareness of what he has discovered in the session. He looks frustrated but agrees and says he wishes to continue to talk to his father in this way next week. 'There's years of stuff I want to tell him.'

Perls Hefferline and Goodman view resistance, as resistance to awareness and resistance to contact. (Perls *et al.*, 1951/94). As we have written earlier, change generates anxiety and therefore a natural self-protective desire to protect against change. This is usually out of awareness and thus creates ambivalence, manifesting in Phillip's as confusion as a consequence of an internal struggle between his conflicting desires – to talk to his father about his deep hurt and his fear of talking to him. This ambivalence to maintain the status quo or behave differently affects Phillip's relationship with himself (his depression as unexpressed and therefore retroflected anger) and with others (his displacement of his anger with his father onto his son). Again we would emphasize that the word resistance implies negative connotations and judgment so we prefer to use instead the term 'creative adjustment' emphasizing the survival component in the process of resistance. It would be a threat to the survival of the child for Phillip to have expressed anger directly to his father. The fantasized or real loss of love from father would have been devastating for him. In situations of ambivalence such as this, which is very similar to the famous top dog under dog polarities described by Perls (ref), the therapist's task is to facilitate awareness of the conflict arising from the polarities and thereby support Phillip to experiment with shifts in understanding, emotion and behaviour that can emerge from increased awareness.

We want to emphasize that two-chair work is about changes in awareness or the emergence of a new gestalt and not simply about catharsis. Awareness impacts not only emotion but cognition and behaviour as well, leading to new understanding and meaning (Greenberg *et al.*, 1988). Two Chair work helped Phillip become aware of competing schematic structures out of awareness. When he became aware of the different thoughts, feelings and behaviours associated with each of the two competing parts of himself and played these out in turn, what emerged was him beginning to make changes in his attitude and behaviour to his father, in the safety of the therapeutic relationship. So when change is desired, a two-chair experiment can switch the focus from the content of change to the process of change. Phillip got stuck with the first experiment because of the content of change, his anger with his father was too threatening and he indeed appeared to regress and disempower himself. When Phillip became aware of the process stopping him from confronting his father, his realization that he feared the loss of his father's love, he re-empowered himself sufficiently to begin to work on the content.

We emphasize the importance of raising awareness and not seeking change itself. If the therapist becomes invested in the client changing in this direction or that, then the therapist will encounter the client's resistance. This is because a split may develop within the client, with the part of them that wants to change being split off and projected onto the therapist. With the therapist invested with the desire for change that part of the client that does not want to change will resist the therapist's attempts to try and do so.

The following week Phillip is eager to return to engaging in cushion work with his father and immediately I notice and draw his attention to his clenched fists.

'Phillip are you aware of what is happening in your hands?'

Phillip stops clenching his fists and looks at his hands and begins to clench and unclench them.

'Phillip I suggest you increase the tension in your fists and allow them to tighten and see what feelings and thoughts emerge, is this ok with you?'

Phillip nods and begins to squeeze his fists into tight balls so that they are white at the knuckles. I draw his attention to his tight jaw and red face and he says, 'Christ I am so bloody angry ... furious in fact ... I ... (he begins to strike the arms of the chair) ... I ...' (he appears stuck for words and continues to hold his fists in two extremely tight balls).

'Phillip if you were to give a voice to your fists what would they say just now?'

'You fucking bastard how dare you ...' Phillip begins to strike the arms of the chair with greater ferocity and I am concerned for his safety. Given his tendency to retroflection he may well express anger and hurt himself at the same time?

'Phillip, I suggest you sit on the floor and address your father directly in the first person present tense and put some of those cushions each side of you so you protect your fists from the impact with the floor?'

Phillip sits on the floor but immediately stretches forward and grabs hold of the large red cushion representing his father and begins to pound it with heavy blows. I check with him that he is not hurting himself and he replies that he is feeling great. I notice that he is pounding the cushion but his mouth is shut tight. Heavy but noiseless pounding is another indication of possible retroflection?

'Phillip is there something you want to say to your father?'

Immediately he begins to speak but there appear so many competing words so I suggest he simply makes a noise. He then lets out a huge roar and pounding the cushion yells and roars abuse at this father for several minutes and then falls forward onto the cushion and begins to cry, sobbing deeply and alternately expressing sadness and anger.

Significantly, Philip eventually emphasizes the anger and deflects the sadness. I support this deflection for now because I am aware that he has a large store of anger which may be repressed if he were to proceed to explore his sadness prematurely. Furthermore, as the later development of the therapy unfolds, it becomes clear it is too soon just now for him to touch the depth of sorrow he will only be able to tolerate later.

For several sessions Phillip eagerly returns to work with his father and identifies several introjects that he believes have profoundly affected his life. In particular he recognizes the competing nature of some messages from his father, for example, 'Get a good education' but 'Don't boast'. 'Education is the thing lad' but 'University graduates have no common sense.' 'Speak properly' but 'Don't sound posh.' Each new insight is accompanied by expressions of pent up anger.

Phillip identifies how much he has betrayed his own desires in order to please his father and avoid criticism. He realizes that he let go of his interest in photography because it was devalued by his father as being unproductive and a waste of time. He never dared share with anyone in the family, except his brother, of his interest in Buddhism. Any mention of his interest in nature and wildlife, he realized would have been similarly despised as a waste of time.

Phillip recognizes how much he has repressed his emotional life for fear of being seen as 'less than a man', and begins to realize some of the cost in terms of his availability for intimacy. With puzzled expression Phillip tells me, 'It's like 'I've always known these things but ... somehow never let myself know I knew them?' 'In my experience people need support and permission to accept reality Phillip.' After a minute or so of silent reflection Phillip remarks, 'Yes it's difficult to see things as they really are ... without someone to stand by you.' Phillip seems barely aware of the significance of this latter remark, but I note it and reflect on whether this may signal the transition to the I–Thou phase of therapy?

For the most part Phillip's increased awareness of the influence of his past on his way of being in the world, are accompanied by expressions of incredulity and anger with a degree of sadness emerging but still largely deflected and retroflected. The first year of therapy has seen shifts in Phillip's life outside of therapy. He apologizes to his son for his loosing his temper and after an initial response of shock to this first ever apology from his father, Mark discharges quite a lot of pent up anger toward his father. Phillip was pleased with himself that he managed to hear and contain this, without losing his temper, even though 'some of it was OTT and nothing to do with him' adding sheepishly, 'but most of it was well deserved'. Evelyn also took courage from this to express her fear of his anger over the years and this has led to them starting to talk more. Both are attending an evening class on photography.

For six months, Phillip has been working two days a week as the accountant for a regional wildlife trust. He appreciates the combination of contributing his professional skills with 'doing something worthwhile', though he identified his need 'for still a lot more challenge' in his professional life.

Around 13 months into therapy Phillip proudly told me that together with Evelyn, and Mark he had reluctantly attended his father's company's annual dinner. There he had spontaneously defended his brother-in-law, after his sister had humiliated her husband in front of several members of the family for some innocuous remark. His father had been about to turn on him, when Phillip cut him short and loudly exclaimed, 'Don't you start father, she is only following the example set by you.' Phillip then promptly got up from the table and went to the bar, followed by his brother-in-law. A moment later Mark joined them, grinning widely from ear to ear, and they all had a drink together. Phillip's sister and father did not speak to him the rest of the evening or since, and he said rather triumphantly, 'Do you know, I don't give a damn!' and added, 'Evelyn was shocked but pleased that at last someone had stood up to Arthur.'

8 Interpersonal focus – 'I–Thou' relationship

For three weeks following this incident at the annual dinner Phillip had expressed considerable satisfaction in therapy about his confrontation with his father. He then arrived at the next session and after further expressions of satisfaction announced somewhat hesitatingly at the end of the session, that he thought perhaps now was the time to end therapy? He had been taking stock of all he had learned, was appreciative of my support and was 'now ready to get on with his life'.

We are often supportive of clients who, after a period of ego-building and consequent enhanced self entitlement, wish to end therapy without proceeding further to deeper levels of engagement within the therapeutic relationship. Indeed the wish to continue to engage a client in therapy may reflect the needs of the therapist rather than those of the client? Alternatively, therapist adherence to dogmatic assertions about the nature and duration of therapy (we know best) mean that clients comply with our overt or subtle insistence of such? Certainly, Phillip is capable of consolidating his learning and transferring his learning in therapy to a wider range of issues than those he has focused on, so that a level of ongoing self-directed growth is likely to continue.

The session ended with us agreeing to focus attention on the question of ending next time and as he was leaving Phillip looked anxious. My emotional reaction was both disappointment and fear and I speculated that while my experience of disappointment was likely shared with Phillip, reflecting both my own and Phillip's sense of disappointment, the experience of fear was largely Phillip's. My intuition was that Philip's wish to end therapy was resistance and I further intuited that it may be a recycling of his need for self-sufficiency and, therefore, a move to a false autonomy? But why was this emerging again at this time and after recently successfully establishing greater autonomy from his father? Clearly some significant developmental issue was emerging in the transference to do with Phillip's relationship with me and connected with his relationship with his father. I decided not to speculate further and risk contaminating the next session with my own more specific interpretations which would be antithetical to the I–Thou endeavour. In such situations our clinical experience suggests it is sufficient to trust the process and suspend details about content, which might be premature and unhelpful at this crucial potential turning point in therapy.

Phillip was shifting the focus of therapy from issues 'out there' to his relationship with me, and as such this may be a signal that he is ready to move into the I–Thou phase of therapy, when the focus of therapy is the therapeutic relationship. While it is common for clients to shift the focus of therapy to the relationship with the therapist at some point, they usually do not know how to effect this change, and may often attempt to do so in ways that appear contrary to their underlying need. Here the therapist can model an essential characteristic of I–Thou phase of therapy, the capacity for self-disclosure.

I–Thou contact requires sufficient maturity to self-disclose without trying to control the outcome. This 'commitment to the between' may occur when both therapist and client can speak what is figural, in the hope that the other will receive it and reciprocate with whatever is figural for them (Friedman, 2002, pp. 7–36). This is very different from a response of resistance when the other replies confluently (symbiotically) with what they think you want to hear, or defensively by receding, through various strategies, into isolation rather than engagement.

Phillip's behaviour during and at the end of the session especially his anxiety as he left evoked what we believe were reciprocal experiences in the therapist, namely disappointment and fear. The real issue here is not the therapist's emotions in response to Phillip but rather if these emotions are useful, or harmful, to the therapeutic endeavour? Similarly, the therapist's disclosure of his counter-transference feelings to Phillip may be helpful in facilitating awareness of the underlying process and may even assist Phillip confronting and changing some basic behaviour patterns in relating to others (Keisler, 1988).

Furthermore, the modelling of healthy self-disclosure may be in response to an initiating self–object transference whereby the client is, out of his awareness, seeking help as to how to proceed with something (developmental deficit) that he has simply never been taught?

At the commencement of the next session Phillip looked awkward and anxious and remarked,

Phillip, 'So how does therapy end? Is there a way of doing it?'

Therapist, 'Is that what you really want Phillip?'

Phillip, 'Well we have to end sometime, don't we?'

Therapist, 'You seem less sure this week'

Phillip, 'Well ... what do you think ... I mean ... do you think I should end?'

Therapist, 'Phillip I would like to share with you what I feel as I anticipate our ending therapy.'

Phillip looks anxious 'ok'.

Therapist, 'Phillip you are perfectly entitled to end therapy if that is what you want and I will support you to do so (he looks sad) and I imagine there is still work you could do in therapy. I have feelings of disappointment at not continuing to work with you and some sadness also. We have been working together now for some 14 months'.

Phillip's face lights up and then he tears up and says, 'I thought now I had stood up to my father that was it, I had had my time and I didn't know if it was ok with you for me to keep coming here, whether you wanted to ... ?'

Therapist exploring the counter-transference of fear I enquire 'Are you frightened Phillip?'

Phillip, 'Well ... it's strange you should know that, but since I stood up to dad I have kind of felt lost somehow, I figured I should be happy about it but I think I do feel afraid or maybe just unsure. It's like a big hole has opened up in here ... (points to his stomach) and I feel sort of empty ... ?'

Phillip has responded to my invitation to contact and is speaking with openness and vulnerability and with far less apparent resistance, although I notice he has not spoken of feeling sad, even though he appears sad and he is pulling this counter-transference response in me.

Over the next few months Phillip makes several positive references to how he experiences me as understanding and intelligent, supportive and non-judgemental and eventually tells me, rather shyly, that I am the kind of person he would have liked to have as a father. In parallel with this developing idealization of the therapist he slowly recognizes that in standing up to his actual father he has given up hope that his father will ever give him what he needs. He becomes aware that his former maintenance of the status quo with his bullying father, together with the accompanying repression of his anger towards him, served to protect Phillip from the awareness that his father '... has never been there for me and can never give me what I need'. He expresses considerable anger at this, but sadness continues to be repressed.

A significant development occurred about two years into therapy when Phillip told me he had called his brother, not knowing why exactly and fearful that he might be angry with me. 'After all I have been really critical of him over the years, so I was anticipating being told to "piss off". I think he was kind of shocked at first and wary of me but he quickly became very friendly and said he was delighted I had contacted him. He enquired after my part-time work at the wildlife trust telling me Mark had told him about it and also about the confrontation with father at the annual bash. He said 'Well done mate', and added, 'not before bloody time'. It's amazing but he is a member of his regional wildlife trust and involved in Greenpeace.'

Phillip was talking animatedly and with enthusiasm about his brother and continued, 'When we were kids we were pretty close for a while, and I've found myself thinking about him and me when we were young. He was a rebel even then and always rubbing father up the wrong way'.

Phillip is quiet and thoughtfully reflecting on the past and after a while he says, in a whisper, 'I saw him get beaten a lot ... I couldn't help him, I just stood there'.

Therapist, 'tell me some more about what that was like for you Phillip, to witness your brother get beaten'.

Here I am experiencing a profound sadness in the countertransference. Some of this is natural compassion and empathy and some reciprocal counter-transference. Phillip looks profoundly sad and is very still and quiet.

Therapist (supporting the mirroring self–object transference), 'Phillip it must have been really tough for you to have to see that, to witness the beating?'

At this point there is a dramatic physical change in Phillip's presence, from a sad slumped body posture to an erect and rigid position and with a face contorted with rage and disdain and with a look of thunder he sneers at me and shouts at me, 'You haven't a fucking clue what it was like for me' and with a dismissive gesture of his hand he goes on, 'you're talking a load of therapist clap trap, what do you know?' He looks aloof and defiant and I am deeply impacted by what I experience as an attack. I imagine I experience something of what it must have been like for him as a child – sarcasm, dismissal, humiliation and a deep sense of being 'wiped out'. Momentarily, I lose my thinking and am confused and fearful, as I imagine he often must have been as a child. I rely on my clinical experience and trust the process replying first with a description of what just happened, followed by a self-disclosure of my experience and, with the gradual re-emergence of my thinking, I end with an important question delivered to try and enhance Phillip's awareness of what is being repeated from history in the here-and-now of the therapeutic relationship.

Therapist, 'Phillip, I was listening intently to you talk about your father beating up on your brother, and feeling a lot of compassion I reached out to you in your obvious distress. I then experienced you responding to me with sarcasm and angry disdain, which impacted me deeply. I experienced being dismissed by you and feel unseen, fearful and angry. I want to ask you "Who did this to you"?'

Phillip's posture instantly deflated, as did his seething anger, and with eyes filled with tears he replied sorrowfully, 'That's just how it was for me – being dismissed as if I didn't exist and anything I had to say was worthless, worse than worthless and it was so humiliating … so humiliating. Somewhere I feel ashamed for just existing, yes that's it …'

Therapist, 'I understand Phillip, and I don't want you to speak to me in that dismissive way.'

Phillip is silent for a moment or two repeatedly looking at me then looking away and eventually he says, with a sense of shocked awareness 'I've just done to you what he (father) did to me … I am so sorry.'

Therapist, 'Thank you Phillip, I accept your apology and appreciate your insight as to what has just occurred between us.'

We agree with the perspective of Interpersonal Psychotherapy that a therapist may experience within a session the client's distinctive interpersonal problems. The therapist registers the client's distinctive style and central problems through the impact messages he/she experiences with the counter-transference. The therapist's task is not to get hooked into a maladaptive game in the interpersonal encounter. The emotional reactions of the therapist are likely to be shared with others in the client's life (e.g. Mark) and serve as important cues to the client's unsuccessful interpersonal behaviour and are important feedback to the client towards resolving his interpersonal problems (Kiesler, 1996). From our integrative perspective we would argue that any resolution of maladaptive interpersonal behaviour has parallel healing implications in the client's intrapsychic world.

The remainder of the session we focus on the power of shame and Phillip is able to identify with a definition of shame as 'an inner repulsion against one's own existence' (Evans, 1994). Phillip ended the session by recalling the metaphor of Christopher Columbus and remarked, with feeling, Phillip, 'So this is the sailors experience of the storm?' I'm glad you told me that story and I didn't realize at the time just what it might mean. But it makes sense now.

This was a pivotal session in the course of therapy. Phillip resisted my empathic attunement by transferring his child ego onto me and then replayed with me something of his father's behaviour towards him. My reciprocal reactive counter-transference connected with aspects of my own history. When reactive counter-transference connects with proactive counter-transference, then therapist's projective identification is more likely because the therapist becomes more vulnerable to confluence or symbiosis with the client.

In a review of counter-transference Tansey and Burke conclude that the notion of the therapist as a blank screen who maintains neutrality and anonymity is no longer a viable concept. The client will attempt to transform the therapist into a transference object and the counter-transference is always transactional, a joint creation involving contributions from both therapist and client. The therapist's own subjectivity is always involved in the way the client's behaviour is experienced (Tansey and Burke, 1989).

How is a therapist to use such an experience which can result in either therapeutic rupture or potential healing? It is perhaps the most challenging experience facing a therapist to experience this kind of symbiotic identification with the client and use it purposefully? At one level Phillip is inviting rejection and a repetition of history and yet at a deeper level we believe he is seeking some degree of healing of the wounds of history. Essentially we believe Phillip's dismissive response was akin to a challenge to the authenticity and trustworthiness of the therapist thus, 'So you (the therapist) really want to know what it was like for me (the client)? Very well then, take that, I'll show you what it was like to be me'!

The therapist has to find a way to respond that accepts what is being conveyed, despite the sense of personal attack together with the emotional cost that accompanies it, find a way of using the experience to enable the client to become aware of the underlying process, and deliver to the internalized critical parent in the client that this behaviour is not appropriate. We believe that while the process is being played out and the critical parent in the client is actively engaged, it is potentially healing to challenge the internalized parent in the immediacy of the moment when it is more likely to have the maximum impact. Psychologically speaking this encounter was the first time that Phillip (from a place where both the child ego and critical parent are actively engaged) would have experienced anyone standing up to his internalized critical father, and survive! Subsequently, this encounter significantly, disempowered Phillip's internalized critical parent and further strengthened his capacity to live with less of a sense of having to live up to his father's expectations.

Developmentally this encounter was an example of the client's need of the adversarial self–object transference in which the client can enter into a conflict with the therapist and not get 'wiped out' in the process and thereby repeat history. At the same time it is important that the therapist also does not allow himself to be 'wiped out' in the encounter as this would consolidate the power of the internalized critic in the client at the expense of their child ego, and so also repeat history. The encounter is a necessary power struggle with the client but one in which the therapist models fairness and firmness. This encounter was indeed pivotal in that it also confirmed that Phillip now had sufficient self-support to be challenged, without withdrawing behind a wall of isolation or adaptive compliance.

The I–Thou phase of therapy could be more accurately described as the I–Thou/I–It seesaw as the client swings back and forth between contact and resistance, contact and objectification. The therapist is, alternately, both a necessary transference object and a person, until such time that a fairly consistent pattern of I–Thou mutuality is established. This usually signals the beginning of the end phase of therapy.

In subsequent sessions Philip spoke of his meeting with this brother and remarked 'it was as if the years had rolled away and we were kids again'. Philip identified his jealousy about the quality of the relationship between his brother and Mark, but was also able to hold onto and appreciate his own improving relationship with his son. Phillip shared how he had helped Mark move away from home into a flat in the town and felt supportive of his part-time work with a computer company. To his surprise he had initially responded to Mark's decision to move out with regret and sorrow, 'after all those months of my nagging him to grow up, move out and get a job I felt, oh no not now we're getting on at last ... but we are both involved in the nature conservation group so we'll meet regularly and (grinning widely) his mother is convinced he'll be bringing his washing around each week!'

Following Mark's move into his own flat (some two and half years or so into therapy) Phillip remarked quizzically and sorrowfully, 'Why is it when things are going so well at home with Evelyn and I, and I am enjoying my son and I've found my brother again ... why is it I feel so sad ... sort of empty and lost?'

Therapist, 'Oscar Wilde once said there's only one thing worse than not getting what you want and that's getting what you want.'

Phillip, 'How come?'

Therapist, 'When you get what you want you may realise what you never had!'

Phillip, 'M,m,m like when you saw my distress and I responded like my father by dismissing you?'

Therapist, 'Say some more.'

Phillip, 'Well, if I had felt your concern for me, you're kindness to me ... I would have felt all the lack of warmth from my father?'

Therapist, 'So how does this relate to your feelings of sadness and emptiness when things are going well for you right now, Phillip?'

Phillip, 'Mm ... huh ... well ... my mind's gone blank ... I had it on the tip of my tongue ... hang on a minute ... huh ... yeah ok ... I got it now I think ... huh ... yeah that's it ... I regret all the missed opportunities with Mark when he was young ... huh ... and now my brother and I are rebuilding our relationship ... huh ... and I miss the years I ignored him I guess ... yeah I do ... a lot really.' Phillip looks very sad and makes frequent eye contact with me, checking me out before letting go and letting the tears roll down his face. After a minute or so he goes on, 'It's strange but these tears feel kind of ... I dunno sort of clean somehow ... am I making sense? It's like their ok ... I have good reason to cry ... I miss my son ... and my brother and I ... I ... well ... I love them.' Phillip cries and laughs at the same time.

The following session Phillip came in and spontaneously slid off the chair onto a large floor cushion and with knees tucked up and arms resting on them he begun to reminisce about his early life with his younger brother. 'I have been recalling so many memories huh ... good one's ... huh ... on the whole ...' (at this moment and apparently out of his awareness) he extends his right arm in my direction, resting it on his knee with his hand turned upward and open. As he continues to talk I notice a profound change in my emotional reactions towards him from warmth to irritation. I begin to experience him as whining and whingeing and feel pulled to dismiss and reject him. This of course would be deeply humiliating for him and I realize that his history is figural once again in a potentially negative way. Here, of course, is the opportunity to do something different and respond instead to the underlying developmental deficit.

We consider the possibility of touch in therapy in a similar way to self-disclosure in that it too can be useful or be a hindrance in the therapy. Again there needs to be a theoretical rationale for introducing touch into therapy and in a way that invites permission from the client.

Therapist, 'Phillip I would like to draw your attention to your right hand.'

He looks at his hand and with alarm withdraws it back.

Therapist, 'Phillip I invite you to experiment with placing your hand back in the previous position and tell me what you experience?'

Phillip responds immediately and is silent for a little while and then struggles to say, 'I feel kinda dirty … as if I would contaminate you if I touched you … huh.'

Therapist, I extend my hand towards his and stop a few inches away and say, 'Would you like to try?'

Phillip, 'The short distance between us seems like a thousand miles … I feel pathetic and disgusting … and am finding it hard to look at you.'

Therapist, 'What do you imagine you might see?'

Phillip, 'Well … huh … contempt … no … that's not you … you wouldn't do that … huh … oh …' He moves his hand forward slowly at first and then grabs my hand in his and squeezes tightly but not uncomfortably and begins to cry. I notice he is not looking at me.

Therapist, 'Make eye contact with me Phillip.'

Phillip, slowly turns to look at me with anxious eyes which then soften and he laughs and cries alternately saying 'this feels so good, so damn good and so painful but … please let me hold your hand for a little while yet'.

Therapist, 'Fine you hold my hand and let yourself feel whatever you are feeling Phillip' I become aware that I am feeling protective towards him when he says, Phillip, 'Why didn't she (mother) stop him? Why didn't she tell him? How could she walk away when he was beating my brother and chastising me? What the hell could she have been thinking?'

At this time we believe the merger self–object transference is figural and that the therapist use of touch is appropriate and respectful and meeting an early developmental need for protection and actual physical holding. To withhold physical contact at this point would have been a profound missed opportunity and possibly a repetition of history? I am aware that Phillip has a creative adjustment of anger covering and deflecting sadness.

Therapist, 'Phillip, let yourself feel your sadness. I acknowledge and respect your anger also but just now try and stay with your sadness.'

Phillip 'You're right ... but that's harder ... she didn't look after us.'

Therapist, 'Phillip, 'I invite you to refer to your self in relation to your mother ...'

Phillip, 'ok yeah, she didn't protect me ... she didn't look after me ... I ... I needed her to be kind to me ... to love me ... how could she not do that'? Phillip sobs uncontrollably for several minutes interspersed with remarks of incredulity at his mother's neglect.

For the following six months this theme of maternal neglect occupied most of the therapy and Phillip experienced a time of anguish and a sense of profound loneliness and sorrow culminating in a form of depression typical of the grieving process. Phillip was letting in his history thereby facing the reality that his creative adjustment had hitherto successfully defended against. Consequently, he was confronted by an existential crisis of meaning.

In this situation it was tempting to want to rescue him by moving him on and away from the 'fertile void'. We believe the therapist's task is to stay alongside Phillip and not rob him of his feelings of grief for his lost childhood. It is necessary to trust the process that, paradoxically, by staying with the anguish Phillip would find a way of coming to terms with it. On several occasions over the six months Phillip and I reflected on the 'doldrums experience' in the Columbus story, which was again experienced as a sustaining metaphor for Phillip.

Generally, though certainly not universally, we consider touch during a profound experience of existential anguish as counterproductive, providing inappropriate soothing that is more likely to take him away from his anguish than into it. It could well reflect a failure of empathy on the part of a therapist unable to tolerate the client's anguish. Consistent sustained empathy and staying alongside Phillip models a capacity to tolerate anguish that he may eventually internalize. Premature attempts to soothe or otherwise take him away from this experience would simply parallel the process of avoidance of discomfort and superficiality that has been described as characteristic of contemporary narcissistic culture (Lasch, 1979).

9 'I–Thou' mutuality – the end of the relationship

Ironically Phillip gradually emerged from this process of grief when he returned to the very question he first came into therapy to resolve, namely what work to do? Phillip had long since returned to playing squash with former colleagues at his sports centre and with a mixture of concern for them, together with a little smugness, he told of their dissatisfaction and lack of fulfilment at work. He compared this with his own sense of purpose and motivation but shared his frustration that his employment was only part-time. He said he planned to write a paper for the board regarding the financial and organizational structure of the charity making recommendations for change. He was excited about this but cautious about being seen as presumptuous. He felt strongly that some radical restructuring would strengthen the charity and enable it to fulfil its vision more effectively.

Phillip, 'The real strength of the organization is at local and regional level but views and opinions at this level are not adequately communicated to the Board which is far too remote.'

My sense was that Phillip was 'talking about' rather than focused purposefully and I felt frustrated, so I directed his attention to his relationship with his parents of whom I had learned little in recent weeks. Phillip appeared to move uncomfortably and I surmised I had drawn his attention to a significant area.

Phillip, 'Well ... huh ... I did want to share some thoughts with you about my mum and dad.' I noticed the personal reference to his parents instead of the usual titles, father and mother.

He continues (looking a little phased) 'Well, huh ... yeah ... mum first then. She has been calling around lately ... I mean more than usual. Evelyn's noticed it too. She's making an effort I think and I've found myself reflecting on her life ... things I've gleaned, with some difficulty, over the years.

She doesn't share much about herself … just a few things that have sort of slipped out and Evelyn's picked up a few gems too.'

I notice Phillip is speaking about his mother with none of the hitherto resentment.

Phillip, 'I don't think I have ever told you that she was an only child and … her father was away in the war when she was born. He returned home when she was about three years old. Evelyn found out from her recently that her father was very withdrawn and rarely spoke to her except in anger. He was wounded but I don't know the details. It must have been very hard for her to suddenly find a stranger living in the home? She had to be very quiet apparently, because noise caused him blinding headaches. Poor kid … poor mum.'

Therapist, 'How does this knowledge effect your sense of her now?'

Phillip, 'Mmmm … well … huh … in some ways she seems to have married a man who is also aloof and distant but what I realize is that we are all impacted by our own experiences. Look at the way I treated Mark? That has a lot to do with how my dad treated me. So … I guess … I guess she wasn't protected either was she? Don't get me wrong she still should have protected me and my brother, but … well I can understand her getting on with my sister when I hear what her father was like and then to go and marry my dad on top of that … Christ.'

Therapist, 'Philip, I notice you are referring to both your parents as mum and dad. I think this is the first time you have done this? You normally refer to them, as mother and father? What does this mean for you?'

Phillip, 'Mmm you're right … him too? … Dad? I hadn't realized that until you just mentioned it. Well I'm never going to forgive that bastard for what he's done … (Phillip looks a me defiantly) but you know he had a hell of an upbringing too.'

Therapist, 'Do you want to tell me?'

Phillip, 'Well … maybe … yeah I guess … what I know is that he was the oldest in a very large family, 10 children I think. At least 2 died very young and he left school at 12 or 13 to work down the colliery. The first winter he worked he only saw daylight once a week on his one day off … because he went to work in the dark and came home in the dark. He frequently boasts about his time down the pit and how it made a man of him'. With compassion in his voice he continues, 'the silly bugger ... it must have been a nightmare for a lad of that age'.

After a short silence Phillip looks at me with a quizzical grin and says, 'I got a letter from the golf club secretary enquiring whether I would like to apply for membership ... they are looking to increase their numbers and get some young blood involved ... and you would never believe this but ... (looks at me with incredulity) Evelyn told me on the weekend that mum had said, my dad had put my name forward ... I was ... am ... flabbergasted'!

Therapist, 'What does this mean to you Phillip?'

Phillip, 'Well at first I thought too bloody late mate ... but I have been thinking over the weekend that maybe I can have some sort of relationship with him ... I mean a little better than the one I have. He will never give me what I really need I know that but ... well ... something is better than nothing, don't you think? And he is very cautious around me these days and has stopped his "know it all" crap'.

Therapist, 'What accounts for this change?'

Phillip, 'I think he has woken up to the fact that his grandson and two sons are not going to jump to his tune and that if he wants to see us he needs to show more respect. Otherwise he will end up a lonely old git.' 'And ... I never dreamed ... he could ever make an effort even if it is for his own selfish motives'.

Therapist, 'Is this another reference to Columbus?'

Phillip, thoughtful for a moment or two and then grins and replies, 'You never know what you are going to discover!'

The following week Phillip arrives and says he has a 'bone to pick' with me. I sense an element of good natured teasing in his voice.

Therapist, 'I am curious ... say some more?'

Phillip, 'What we talked about last week was very important for me but it could have waited perhaps until this week, or next perhaps, because I was wanting to talk about something else that was very very important for me last week and you missed me. I realize I am angry with you, and curious as to what was going on for you because I have not experienced you in this way, before?'

The therapist's initial response was to feel angry and defensive followed by shock and then curiosity as Phillip's remarks appeared increasingly appropriate.

Therapist, 'I will take some time to think this through with you Phillip as I sense you are correct and I did miss you, but it's not yet clear to me how I did that ... I recall you expressing concern about the way the charity was organized ... huh ... and that you were considering writing a report or paper perhaps for the board? I then enquired after your parents. I recall feeling frustrated and thought you were avoiding issues to do with your parents ... huh ... now you went on to talk openly about your thoughts and feelings towards them both. I recall you looking uncomfortable and thought it was to do with avoiding talking about them. Were you uncomfortable because I changed the subject and took you away from your agenda?'

Phillip, 'Yeah looking back after the session yeah ... but ... at the time I guess I was confused by your reaction and didn't let myself know that I was pissed off with you for ignoring me. The issue was very important to me and I was excited by the proposals I had thought through for the charity'.

Phillip's mention of feeling excited opened a window for the therapist whose childhood experience included negative messages about showing excitement. Therapist's counter-transference feelings are harmful to the therapeutic process if they remain undetected (Guy and Brady, 2001). In this case the therapist counter-transference reaction represented residual effects of an insufficiently resolved conflict and anxiety. By identifying this the therapist could re-establish a more objective transaction with Phillip (Spotnitz, 1969).

Furthermore, the tendency in psychotherapy to focus exclusively on the past in the present and ignore contemporary cultural issues, especially regarding ecological concerns, provides a convenient platform to deflect therapist resistance into the premature and hasty notion that it was instead the client who was resisting.

Therapist, 'Phillip I appreciate your directness in confronting me about this. I see now that I was the one who was into avoidance. I am also aware of where this originates in my history. I acknowledge that I missed you and ignored what was very important to you and I am sorry that I responded in this way.'

Phillip is thoughtful for about a minute and then is visibly moved to tears and struggling to speak says, 'Thank you, thank you so much ... you see ... (crying but maintaining eye contact) you see ... it means so much ... you see he (father) never once said he was sorry to me ... not once ... not then and not now. This means so much to me ...'

Ironically this 'mistake' on the part of the therapist led to a special moment in the work when the mutuality of contact was of an intense and reciprocal human encounter characterized by honesty, vulnerability and courage on both sides. Neither therapist nor client was controlling the encounter, but rather there was a 'commitment to the between' a willingness to trust the process. As well as a profoundly human experience both client and therapist later reflected on the equally profound sense of having participated in a spiritual encounter. Indeed Lynne Jacobs believes that 'I–Thou' is the highest from of human communication (Jacobs, 1989). We have argued earlier (chapter ...) that such human contact at its most poignant moment can be a meeting of souls.

Whatever one's take on the relationship between the human and the spiritual in this encounter, what is clear is that this marked a degree of horizontality in the therapy that is characteristic of the end stage of therapy. For Phillip to be able to confront the therapist in such a direct, open and mature way requires that he be able to successfully challenge his 'creative adjustment' or defensive patterns. Specifically, this means he is now able to overcome his pattern of retroflecting feelings, projecting them onto others and, most particularly, his hitherto crippling sense of shame and wrongness. He is able to be fully present and practice inclusion towards the therapist. He has also successfully worked through the idealizing self–object transference.

The ending of the therapy occurred some three months later at a mutually agreed time. This was a sad and beautiful parting with Phillip having the last word thus, 'Like Colombus my experience (of therapy) has been painful at times, wonderful at times, and terrifying at times but it has been the best thing I've ever done for me and those I love. Life is still tough, don't get me wrong, bloody tough at times, but I don't feel defeated by it anymore ... I feel liberated from my past ... all things are possible.'

Postscript

Phillip wrote his paper for the board and to our delight he received a positive response and an offer of full-time employment in a newly created post. He accepted it.

10 The parallel process in supervision

We consider the capacity for reflexive practice or 'critical subjectivity' (Reason, 1994) the most important characteristic of the psychotherapist (and supervisor) who has evolved an 'internal supervisor' (Casement, 1985). Reflexive practice requires a delicate holding of an awareness of the therapist's own experience and that of the client, while simultaneously standing back and reflecting on the dynamic interaction between the two. The capacity for reflexive practice is perhaps nowhere more challenged and tested than in the identification, acknowledgment and understanding of the parallel process.

The clinical work with Phillip was the subject of peer supervision with an experienced colleague, on several occasions during the course of therapy. The focus was almost exclusively on the transference, both in the therapist–client relationship and in the therapist–supervisor relationship, as it emerged or was enacted in the parallel process (Doehrman, 1976).

We wish to stress that there are a range of issues for supervision other than simply the parallel process. Indeed an overemphasis on the parallel process, especially for less experienced therapists, could may be experienced as bordering on personal therapy and be somewhat intimidating and oppressive. Elsewhere we have written about the range of possible issues for supervision such as assessment and diagnosis, strategies of intervention, ethics and professional practice concerns, theoretical development, therapist self care and so on (Gilbert and Evans, 2000). However, our relational and development approach to integrative psychotherapy is further explicated through the exploration of the parallel process.

The literature on the parallel process has come largely from the psychoanalytic tradition. Little has been written from within the humanistic and integrative approaches, except some reference to the phenomenon in textbooks on supervision, for example, Carroll, 1996; Hawkins and Shohet, 2000; Gilbert and Evans, 2000. Currently the authors are also aware of an interesting research project exploring the parallel process in supervision from a humanistic perspective, and conducted collaboratively by two integrative psychotherapists and two gestalt psychotherapists (Poole, 2005 (forthcoming)) and due for publication in 2005.

Searles (1955) understood the parallel process as a repetition in supervision of a process initiated in therapy by the client, that is, a unilateral process. Doehrman (1976), however, challenged this traditional understanding when she published research that suggested a process could be initiated in supervision, by the supervisor, and then repeated in the therapy. Others have written about the multi-directional nature of supervision emphasizing that a process can be initiated by client, therapist or supervisor in one context and then repeated in another (Stoltenberg and Delworth, 1986; Ekstein and Wallerstein, 1972).

We perceive the parallel process to be a phenomenon best understood through field theory (Lewin, 1952). Lewin stressed the interrelatedness of the individual with their environment, both their internal world of sensations, feelings, thoughts and the like, and the external world, both animate and inanimate. In order to understand a person it is necessary to understand them in the overall context in which they are situated. The context or field is a dynamic and interrelated system in which every part influences every other part such that everything is connected to everything else. In psychotherapy and in supervision there is thus a co-created field of mutual reciprocal influence between client and psychotherapist in the former, and between psychotherapist and supervisor in the latter. In the context of supervision both systems (therapist–client and therapist–supervisor) overlap so that the current nature of the therapeutic relationship, together with the personal histories of the client, psychotherapist and supervisor will each impact the field. Family therapy has long understood the notion of circular causality where events and explanations are viewed as multi-causal, multi-determined and reciprocal in nature. This perspective, which contrasts markedly with the Newtonian concept of linear cause and effect, encourages consideration of all aspects of the field, past, present and future.

Here we shall discuss examples from the work with Phillip where the parallel process appears, on separate occasions, to have been initiated either by Phillip, or by the psychotherapist or by the supervisor. We do so with curiosity rather than judgment and thus in the spirit of critical reflection. Our view of transference phenomena is influenced by intersubjectvity theory which regards the transference as an instance of a person's 'unconscious organising activity', which is shaped by archaic perceptions of self and others that in turn organize our perception of the world. This is similar to notion in gestalt therapy of 'creative adjustment', which describes the infant's survival choices as the best possible options available to them at the time, but which choices may now be 'out of date' and dysfunctional in the 'here-and-now'. Neither the psychotherapist nor the supervisor are immune from this process, given that each of them will be influenced in their respective professional roles by their personal histories, and by their particular knowledge base in psychology and psychotherapy, which will in turn influence what each chooses to attend to in their respective professional encounters.

The above-mentioned view clearly challenges the psychotherapeutic literature that makes the assumption of the neutrality of the psychotherapist. Following the tradition of Ferenczi (1988), Kohut (1984), Casement (1985), Bollas (1991) and Langs (1994), we hold the view that the countertransference of the psychotherapist is an inevitable, indispensable and invaluable source of information about the process of therapy. Both the psychotherapist and the supervisor will inevitably be influenced by the client's unconscious process and the client, in turn will also be influenced by the unconscious process of both the psychotherapist and the supervisor.

Bollas (1991) writes about the psychotherapist's 'countertransfrence readiness', that is, their openness to their own experience so that they can welcome 'news from within themselves' that comes through their own intuitions, feelings, passing images and fantasies.

Casement (1985) writes of 'communication by impact' to describe the process whereby clients stir up feelings in the psychotherapist that they are unable to communicate in words. The task of the psychotherapist is to tolerate their own pain and confusion and persevere in their attempts to understand what it is the client is trying to communicate.

For us it is more important to understand the meaning underlying any experience of the parallel process rather than be preoccupied with who triggered it, whether that be the client, psychotherapist or supervisor. Indeed from a field-theory perspective can we ever assume, with any real certainty, with whom a process might actually originate? What really matters is the psychotherapist's capacity to reflect on a process, identify what is happening, understand its meaning and significance and find a way to effectively communicate this to the client. This capacity for critical reflection on the process of therapy while remaining open to the influence of oneself on the process, we consider the major characteristic of personal and professional maturity.

What we have come to notice over the years is that the parallel process, time again, tends to pre-empt a 'healing crisis' by which we mean the possibility of change for the client. Our clinical experience supports the view of the intersubjective theorists that there are two dimensions to the transference, which they refer to as the 'self object' and 'repetitive' dimensions (Stolorow and Attwood, 1992, p. 25). As regards the former, the client will look to the psychotherapist to meet some developmental needs. Here the assumption is that the client will heal developmental deficits from childhood through 'internalizing' the psychotherapist's sustained empathy. The latter 'repetitive' dimension refers to the client's fears and expectations that the current experience with the psychotherapist will be a repetition of a developmental failure from their past. These two aspects of the transference often oscillate in the parallel process so that at any moment one may be figural while the other is in the background. It is crucial for the psychotherapist, in reflecting on the meaning of any experience of the parallel process, to understand what developmental deficit(s) may be calling for attention, and in what ways the psychotherapist may be being invited or coerced (Cashdan, 1988) to repeat the client's history.

Therapeutic 'mistakes' occur when the psychotherapist repeats the client's history. However, these often appear to us to be necessary 'errors', to the extent that they appear indispensable for discovering the underlying meaning of the process for the client. How the psychotherapist then deals with the 'mistake' will be crucial to the experience of healing.

Peer supervision 1

In this supervision session with an experienced colleague, Phillip did not appear to be figural at all, and I (psychotherapist) became aware of feeling ambivalent and tired about discussing any client work, until my colleague (peer supervisor) expressed their irritation with me for not being very present and seemingly preoccupied. It was only then that I became aware of my ambivalence about bringing a new client, Phillip, to supervision. In introducing Phillip to my colleague I also experienced, in turn, irritation with Phillip because of his seeming ambivalence about his commitment to therapy. With this realization of the parallel process the session immediately became more energetic.

Initial exploration centred on the polarities in my emotional experience of Phillip oscillating between anger, with a desire to humiliate him, in response to his arrogant and passive aggressive presentation. Alternatively I experienced a warmth and tenderness towards him when I intuited an underlying yearning for contact. I shared my concern with my colleague as to whether or not Phillip would return to therapy, given my decision to challenge him at a deeper level than his seeming preoccupation with employment. My colleague expressed surprise at the depth of this concern which appeared to contain some considerable anxiety. I was asked to consider who Phillip, in his passive aggressive mode, might represent for me. I immediately became aware of the similarities between his critical and overbearing father and my experience of my own father, who at times could be highly critical. In the transference Phillip was inviting rejection through his aggressive and dismissive behaviour. My initial reluctance to present Phillip in the supervision, reflected a degree of confluence with him in our shared unconscious reluctance about a more powerful engagement with the deeper issues. This awareness was crucial to the second session with Phillip enabling me to stay out of critical parent and model responsibility for the lack of clarity in our contract, together with my expression of interest in him as a person, over and above the issue of employment. Phillip had likely anticipated a power struggle in the follow-up second session, but in the absence of such a struggle he dropped his passive aggressive presentation and we began to build a therapeutic alliance.

Peer supervision 2

Some 10 months into the work Phillip arrived in a highly distressed state having had a row with his son Mark. He acknowledged to me that he had behaved as his father, arrogant, overbearing and dismissive. Phillip experimented in the session with talking directly to his father, represented as a cushion. While engaging in this experiment Phillip began to display common physical signs of anger – clenched fists and tight jaw. I brought the session to an end agreeing to his request to support him to continue to express his anger the following week. The session only had 10 minutes to run and I thought safety was a prime concern. However, in peer supervision my colleague queried my decision, expressed the opinion that Phillip has missed an opportunity to address his anger towards his father, and that he would now be unlikely to be able to return to his anger in the immediate future? We discussed the possibility that my anxiety about my anger towards my own father may have contaminated the process? This did not 'ring true' for me and I remained content with my decision to give priority to client safety.

It was later in our peer supervision, after we had each shared other client work, that my colleague returned to Phillip and acknowledged his own process had 'got in the way'. He recalled being strongly challenged many years ago, in a large training group, about his reluctance to support a peer trainee to express anger. This had been quite humiliating for him and he realized now how much he had 'swallowed whole' that unpleasant experience. Something in my work with Phillip had triggered the humiliation experienced by my colleague all those years ago, which had now been re-played or re-enacted with me, albeit in a more subtle manner. I became aware that I had indeed experienced some sense of embarrassment (parallel process) when confronted by my colleague and had wondered momentarily whether I had 'got it wrong', even though I concluded that I had been content with the appropriateness of putting my client's safety first. Thus an unconscious dynamic had once again been enacted in the parallel process, this time apparently triggered by the supervisor? We both became more acutely aware of the depth of humiliation experienced by Phillip in his relationship with his father, past and present and that this would likely emerge again very strongly in the therapy at some point (see peer supervision 4).

Peer supervision 3

About 14 months into therapy Phillip announced that it was probably time to end therapy because he had sorted out his employment situation and 'stood up to' his father and challenged him publicly. In the peer supervision Phillip was not 'top of my agenda' there being another client I wished to discuss first? However, during the presentation of this other client my colleague became aware of feeling anxious and fearful. We were both perplexed as to the meaning of this because it simply did not appear relevant to the client I was presenting. As the session continued I subsequently shared the current state of play with Phillip and then the 'penny dropped' as we both became aware that Phillip was likely feeling afraid that the therapy might end, despite his apparent suggestion.

I had ended the previous session with Phillip suggesting that we discuss the issue of ending the following week. I had already thought through my response to Phillip and had decided to support him to end if he persisted, but nevertheless model emotional literacy and share my sadness, whilst also sharing my opinion that there was more work he might fruitfully do? Whatever the outcome I thought I was content to finish?

My colleague invited me to explore to what extent I was fearful of modelling the process and sharing my sadness? Was I anxious perhaps lest I experience rejection from Phillip's introjected critical father? I became aware that while I was anxious about Phillip's response I was also intuiting something more, some deeper level of fear not connected directly with fathers, his or mine!

My colleague invited me to put my father on a cushion and talk directly to him. When I did so I was not surprised to immediately experience feelings of sadness and anxiety that the likely response would be that of disdain. However, I still intuited there was something else that was on the very edge of my awareness. My colleague intuitively asked, 'What about your mother?' Then the 'penny dropped'. She always supported her husband, my father, and from what Phillip had told me this was the case with his mother also. So the open expression of feelings was not supported by either of Phillip's parents, nor my own so it was hardly surprising that I was anxious about sharing my sadness with Phillip.

The following week, in a carefully monitored and restrained manner, I shared my sadness about the prospect of ending therapy. Phillip 'teared up' and shared his relief. He had imagined that I would want him to end now that he had stood up to his father, thus finishing the work. With the insight from the previous peer supervision I enquired whether Phillip was frightened at the prospect of therapy ending at this point and he acknowledged that he was. Later in the course of therapy this current work helped to enable Phillip to address the lack of protection he experienced from his mother, both as a child and adult.

Peer supervision 4

In this peer supervision session I had intended only to make a brief reference to what had been a highly significant session with Phillip, where he had responded with a dismissive arrogance and disdain to my empathic support for his experience as a child, when he witnessed his father ruthlessly beat his younger brother. My physical reaction to Phillip's behaviour towards me was to feel as if I had been 'kicked by a mule' in the solar plexus, and I felt humiliated and angry. Phillip heard my healthy protest and my inquiry as to 'who had done this to him'? He was deeply impacted and realized that he had done to me what his father had done to him. Simply acknowledging this as a helpful session, I wanted to move on and discuss another client. My colleague and I did indeed move on to discuss another client when, after a few minutes, he remarked that there was something left over for him from the report of my work with Phillip that he could not quite put his finger on? My immediate response was to express impatience and a desire to move on, to which my colleague replied that he felt there was a process going on and challenged me to reflect on my impatience. Immediately I pictured my father impatiently moving from the successful completion of one task to the next, seemingly without ever stopping to allow himself, or anyone else, to stop and rest and celebrate. I realized I could have responded far more generously to Phillip's courageous and growing capacity for insight and his increased ability to acknowledge his process. I had become caught up in an unconscious process. Phillip's father is similarly impatient, lacking in generosity and focused exclusively on what he perceives others 'get wrong' rather than what others 'get right'.

Peer supervision 5

Towards the end of the therapy Phillip informed me that he had found the 'job of his dreams' where he could combine his skills in accountancy with his commitment to a green ecology. I 'missed him' when I switched the focus of therapy too quickly from his excitement about his new job to the reaction of his parents to his news? The following week Phillip challenged me by expressing his anger with me in a clear and straightforward manner and enquired what had been going on for me last week? Momentarily defensive I took time to think through my reaction and responded with a creative and carefully thought out self-disclosure. I confirmed to Phillip that he was indeed correct. I acknowledged it was to do with issues from my life rather than his. I shared my appreciation of the clear way in which he had expressed his anger and I apologized to him. The impact of my apology was immense and very different from his experience with his father.

Phillip was visibly moved and able to see and acknowledge the juxtaposition between his experience of me and that with his father. The apology corrected the 'therapeutic rupture' from the previous week but also further conveyed a sense of authenticity to our therapeutic endeavour. I modelled the process of healthy contact rather than get caught up in a parallel process of self-justification. What I came to realize as I reflected on my reaction to Phillip's new job in the last session, was an unhealthy fear of excitement in my own family of origin which was being replayed in the process between us. I now took the opportunity of peer supervision to celebrate the efficacy of my self-disclosure in the session with Phillip and share my excitement at the changes he had made in his personal and professional life during his engagement with therapy.

This particular session with Phillip impresses us as a further reminder that progress and healing can evolve out of an apparent therapeutic 'error' and raises the question, was this simply a case of therapist personal history 'getting in the way'? Given that Phillip had been in therapy for three years or more he will have come to 'know' the therapist at a deep level. That being so he may have unconsciously 'set up' the 'error' with the possibility of repeating his own history and/or with the hope of the reparative response he actually received.

It remains unclear who it is that may trigger an unconscious process in psychotherapy, the client, the psychotherapist or the supervisor? We think it is likely always a co-creation at some level. What appears more important and more relevant to the therapeutic endeavour is that the psychotherapist develop his/her capacity and willingness to reflect on the process in as transparent a way as possible. The purpose of this is to reflect on the underlying meaning of the unconscious dynamic being re-enacted in the parallel process and find creative ways of enabling the client to become aware of the significance of the process for themselves.

Part 4

Challenges and concerns

11 Training integrative psychotherapists

We begin this chapter on the training of integrative psychotherapists by first establishing the context within which contemporary training takes place, with particular reference to those training organizations and professional accrediting bodies relevant to integrative psychotherapy. We then outline a coherent conceptual frame for the practice of integrative psychotherapy that provides the basic framework for a training programme. We conclude the chapter with a suggested set of core competencies for the integrative psychotherapist that we believe needs to inform the curriculum content of any training programme in integrative psychotherapy.

The Society for the Exploration of Psychotherapy Integration (SEPI) was formed in 1983 and is an interdisciplinary organization of professionals interested in approaches to psychotherapy that are not limited by a single orientation. It is an international organization with members in many countries. SEPI has hosted some 20 conferences (to 2004) the hallmark of which has been dialogue through participants listening to others as well as sharing their own opinions in a non-dogmatic manner. SEPI has an official journal – *The Journal of Psychotherapy Integration* – which publishes papers that intend to integrate knowledge of psychotherapy and behaviour change with developments in the broader fields of psychology and psychiatry. SEPI can be contacted online.

Interest in psychotherapy integration is at least 70 years old but has grown quite dramatically over the past 20 years or so. Consequently many experienced clinicians trained originally in a single-school approach now consider themselves to be integrative psychotherapists.

However, in recent years there has also been a significant growth in the number of training organizations offering specific programmes in integrative psychotherapy, both in the United Kingdom and in several other European countries. This growth led to the creation of the European Association for Integrative Psychotherapy (EAIP) in 1993, which shortly after in 1996, was among the first of the approaches to psychotherapy to become accredited as a European wide 'school' within the European Association for Psychotherapy (EAP). Integrative psychotherapists who have graduated with a training organization that is a member of the EAIP are eligible for the European Certificate of Psychotherapy (ECP) sponsored by the EAP, which is the professional umbrella body for a wide range of schools of psychotherapy in Europe. The EAP currently (2004) has organizational members in some 26 European nations representing approximately 50,000 psychotherapists.

The EAIP believes that no single school of therapy has a monopoly on 'truth' or 'legitimacy' and has therefore supported and encouraged different forms of psychotherapy integration. Within the EAIP there are different integrative training programmes, for example, humanistic and psychoanalytic, psychodynamic and body process, dialogic and intersubjectivity and so on. In this way the EAIP has successfully avoided integrative psychotherapy developing into yet another single-school approach.

Currently, the EAIP has member organizations in Croatia, Denmark, France, Germany, Greece, Ireland, Italy, Sweden, The Netherlands and the United Kingdom, and prospective members in Russia and Poland. The EAIP welcomes inquiries from organizations in psychotherapy who offer an integrative training programme which is a principled attempt to synthesize two or more approaches to psychotherapy at the theoretical level and resulting in coherent and ethical clinical application.

The founding President of the EAIP was Ken Evans (1995), followed by Maria Gilbert (1998). The current President is Jean-Michel Fourcade who lives and works in Paris, France.

In the United Kingdom, several organizations provide training programmes in integrative psychotherapy which are accredited by the United Kingdom Council for Psychotherapy (UKCP). The UKCP is the professional accreditation body for psychotherapy in the United Kingdom with some 80 organizational members representing a wide range of psychotherapy approaches. In 2003 the UKCP published the 10th anniversary edition of the National Register of Psychotherapists containing over 5,000 registrants.

We shall provide, in alphabetical order, a list of training organizations in the United Kingdom that provide a training in integrative psychotherapy accredited by the UKCP. Those organizations marked with an asterisk are also members of the EAIP.

Bath Centre for Psychotherapy and Counselling
1 Walcot Terrace, London Road, Bath, BA1 6AB
01225 429720
bcpc@ukonline.co.uk

Institute for Arts and Therapy in Education
2-18 Brittania Row, London N1 8PA
020 7704 2534
www.arts-therapy.demon.co.uk

*London Association of Primal Therapists
West Hill House, 6 Swains Lane, London N6 6QU
020 7267 9616
www.lap.org

*Metanoia Institute
13 North Common Road, London W5 2QB
020 8579 2505
www.metanoia.ac.uk

*Minister Centre
Mapesbury Lodge, 17 Mapesbury Road, London NW2 4HU
020 8450 3311
www.os94.dial.pipex.com

Northern Guild for Psychotherapy
83 Jesmond Road, Jesmond, Newcastle NE2 1NH
0191 209 8383
www.northern-guild.co.uk

Regent's College School of Psychotherapy and Counselling
Inner Circle, Regent's Park, London SE1 2TH

020 7487 7406
www.spc.ac.uk

*Scarborough Psychotherapy Training Institute
117 Columbus Ravine, Scarborough YO12 7QU
01723 376 246
www.scpti.co.uk

*Sherwood Psychotherapy Training Institute
2 St James Terrace, Nottingham NG1 6FW
0115 924 3994
www.spti.net

To foster the development of integrative psychotherapy within the United Kingdom, the United Kingdom Association for Psychotherapy Integration (UKAPI) was established in October 1999 with Maria Gilbert as its founding Chair. The main aim of the organization was to provide a 'home' for integrative psychotherapists in this country, with links abroad. An one-day inaugural conference was held at that time. Subsequently, UKAPI held a highly successful two-day joint conference with the EAIP in London in September 2001. Among its aims was the promotion of good practice in integrative psychotherapy, and to this end it fulfils a continuing professional development function. In addition to a second conference in 2004, UKAPI sponsors regular workshops and seminars. UKAPI is now a member organization and is shortly to publish the first issue of its journal: *The British Journal of Psychotherapy Integration*. Further information is available on the UKAPI website: www. ukapi.com.

Thus within a few short years integrative psychotherapy has developed a professional and political structure within Europe. We believe this will help to further the identity of integrative psychotherapy, consolidate its position within the profession and encourage and sponsor ongoing research and development.

Having established the context for integrative psychotherapy in Europe we now consider first the conceptual frame and then the core competencies of the integrative practitioner that need to be addressed during training, and further assimilated through reflexive practice and continued professional development throughout one's professional lifetime.

Conceptual frame

In our opinion any model of integration needs to offer a coherent conceptual framework that reflects a consistency between philosophy, theory and practice. Mahrer (1989) outlines what in his view are the components of a theory of psychotherapy, namely: a theory of human beings; a theory of psychotherapy (description of the key components like therapeutic goals, general strategies etc.); and the concrete operations engaged upon by the therapist. Following Mahrer we have built on this model to form a template for articulating a framework for integration.

In our training programmes and in our supervision of integrative psychotherapists we initially encourage the therapist to review the values and philosophical assumptions underlying clinical practice since these will inform all aspects of the work with clients. These values will of course differ from person to person and also the emphasis will be highly individual.

We then guide the therapist to give a description of their view of the person – the concepts and terms they use to describe functioning (conscious and unconscious). For many this will involve a holistic view of the person in context, but the actual concepts involved will depend on the therapist's interests and perspective. A discussion of motivational forces forms part of the discussion of the person and relate directly to their view of the therapeutic process and the process of change. In our experience therapists tend to stress certain motivational forces that they consider central to their own integrative model. This usually leads on to the inclusion of a developmental perspective on the person showing the difference between optimal and less than optimal developmental sequences. Here again the therapist will draw on those developmental theories that they consider to support their practice. Clearly it is vital that the therapist be able to articulate their view of pathology/dysfunction/diagnosis and to give the main concepts that inform their case conceptualizations of clients.

Fundamental to the training of integrative psychotherapists is the assimilation of the process of psychotherapy itself, that is, how the therapist views the therapeutic relationship, the stages of therapy from inception to termination and the process between therapist and client. What happens in the room between therapist and client and how this is viewed and understood is a central discussion here. This will include some review of the techniques and strategies used by the therapist in the context of the therapeutic relationship as well as a view of the process of change and the factors that the therapist considers make for change in therapy. In the process of developing a framework, we encourage the therapist to draw on contemporary research, inter alia, into areas such as psychotherapy outcome research, research into child and adult development and currently also into neurobiology to support the framework. We equally encourage students to draw on clinical wisdom in the field that is embedded in the many texts describing casework with clients. Based on the above-mentioned frame we can now proceed to fill out some of how this may be translated into the actual practice of integrative psychotherapy in the form of the core competencies suggested.

Core competencies

We believe the following core competencies in integrative psychotherapy are the first attempt to publish one such in the United Kingdom and we offer them solely with the intention of stimulating discussion among our contemporaries and not in any way as a definitive list. The following and concluding chapter will include, among other issues, the statutory regulation of psychotherapy in the United Kingdom, which is closely linked with the issue of professional competency.

We have organized the core competencies under eight key areas and acknowledge that we have been influenced by our involvement in with work undertaken by the UKCP in this area in the late 1990s.

● The purpose of integrative psychotherapy
● What the process of integrative psychotherapy involves

- Carrying out an initial assessment
- Creating and maintaining the working alliance
- Using the therapeutic relationship
- Working through issues
- Working through endings

We are indebted to our training colleagues and students who over a three-year period discussed, amended and eventually agreed the competencies (discussed later) are very much a 'work in progress'. It represents an early stage in the task of establishing and clarifying professional competence in integrative psychotherapy. More will need to be done by the integrative community at large to amend and refine the work, over time and in the light of developing understanding and new knowledge.

The purpose of integrative psychotherapy is

- To participate in the development towards psychotherapy integration
- To form a coherent theoretical integrative synthesis (of relational and developmental models and the findings of outcome research) and to evaluate their application to clinical practice
- To focus particularly on the dynamics and potential of human relationships with the consequent facilitation of the client's possibilities to create and sustain more satisfying relationships
- To facilitate the client towards integration of self

The process of integrative psychotherapy involves

- Understanding the internal and external barriers that people create to the formation of satisfying relationships
- Understanding how these barriers relate to the problems the person experiences
- Engaging the person in a therapeutic relationship which provides the opportunity and therapeutic space for engaging with these relationship problems

*The competent integrative psychotherapists
needs to be able to*

- Make a professional assessment and diagnosis compatible with the theoretical basis of integrative psychotherapy
- Be able to monitor and evaluate the progress of therapy
- Use their theoretical and personal skills and be sensitive and aware of their own contribution to the relationship
- Create a context of safety by ensuring and taking care of the professional boundaries
- Manage self and other in the therapeutic process via self-awareness, honesty, receptivity, professional acceptance and ethical endeavour
- Be available for contact with the client through affective attunement, inclusion and presence and use the counter-transference creatively and ethically
- Use their counter-transference to assist in making sense of early relational confusion in the client
- Transfer learning about the client's past relationships to current functioning
- Be sensitive to the emergence of the transference and address this process in the work
- Examine their own capacity for relationship and reflect on these processes
- Reflect on and conceptualize clinical issues
- Commit to continued professional development
- Identify and seek to repair therapeutic rupture
- Recognize own prejudices
- Recognize limits to own competence
- Recognize the need for supervision, personal therapy, further professional development
- Accommodate own needs outside of the therapeutic relationship
- Work within the ethical standards of the profession

*When conducting initial assessment the competent
practitioner is able to*

- Establish rapport
- Elicit relevant background information, for example, medical, socio-cultural/transcultural factors

- Assess the nature and scale of the problems, difficulties in the intrapsychic process of the client and in their interpersonal functioning
- Assess the degree of ego strength/self-support and evaluate the client's
- Cross reference with a standard mental health classification where appropriate and take expert advice, where appropriate
- Asses the client's potential to form a therapeutic alliance – motivation, capacity, commitment, psychological mindedness/capacity for insight
- Provide information about the nature of integrative psychotherapy
- Instill a measure of hope
- Recognize contra-indications for therapy
- Evaluate therapist–client 'match' and determine whether to refer on

In creating and maintaining the working alliance the competent practitioner is able to

- Establish and maintain a reliable and consistent therapeutic frame based on their integrative approach by collaboratively establishing the therapeutic contract with regard to the nature of therapy, issues of confidentiality, cost, duration, sickness, absence and notice of termination; modelling good time keeping
- Respectfully confront challenges to the therapeutic frame via missed appointments, lateness and non-payment of fees where applicable
- Maintain satisfactory records and in a safe place
- Operate within a recognized professional code of ethics
- Assist the client to explore and become aware of their cognitive, emotional and behavioural functioning
- Facilitate the client to identify connections between early developmental deficits and current relational patterns
- Instil hope in the possibility of change
- Recognize grounds for terminating therapy or referring the client on

*In the use of the therapeutic relationship
the competent practitioner is able to*

- Communicate empathically with the client
- Validate and confirm the client's reality, past and present
- Tolerate, confirm and normalize seemingly overwhelming thoughts and feelings in the client and in self
- Work at a pace the client can tolerate
- Maintain hope in the therapeutic endeavour
- Formulate the client's issues/problems in terms of integrative psychotherapy
- Anticipate and predict, in general terms, the possible direction of therapy
- Facilitate the therapeutic relationship by being available for contact, practicing inclusion and presence, remaining affectively attuned and using the counter-transference responses creatively to assist client to new insight
- Use the counter-transference to understand the impact of the client's history on their 'here-and-now' relating in the therapy room and in the world outside the therapy room
- Identify developmental deficits and effectively contain and manage any healthy dependency
- Recognize and repair therapeutic ruptures
- Respectfully confront the client's defences as appropriate to their level of self-support
- Facilitate the client to appreciate their defences as survival strategies
- Facilitate the client to deeper levels of self-acceptance and self-compassion
- Maintain an respectful attitude towards the client, consistent with the values of integrative psychotherapy
- Recognize and work with the transference and the emergence of unconscious processes in the therapy

*In working through issues the competent
practitioner is able to*

- Accept the client's resistance as their way of making sense of the world, including the world of the therapy room

- Support the client to respect their defences as creative adjustments and
- to work with the transference issues as these unfold
- Adopt a consistent empathic (inclusive) stance that confronts any early negative infant caregiver pattern of relating
- Provide an emotionally reparative relationship, over time
- Establish a contract with client regarding safety of self and others
- Evaluate the social support network within and beyond the client's immediate family
- Regularly reflect on the appropriateness and effectiveness of strategies of intervention/techniques and make effective use of supervision
- Respectfully challenge dysfunctional behaviour

In working through endings the competent practitioner is able to

- Manage premature endings
- Allow sufficient time for endings (e.g. four weeks plus one week for every year of therapy)
- Recognize and challenge denial of ending
- Manage and contain separation anxiety
- Acknowledge 'loss'
- Review the therapeutic journey (recall, reminisce, regret, celebrate)
- Evaluate effectiveness of therapy in relation to client's initial and ongoing expectations
- Model emotional literacy by giving 'permission' to grieve
- Model separation by giving 'permission' to let go and look to the future
- Recognize the impact of previous unsatisfactory endings/ losses in client's experience and respectfully confront repetition
- Recognize and respectfully confront regression as an avoidance of ending
- Recognize and accept when the ending is therapist-led and premature and consider a re-negotiation

● Seek supervision if the therapist finds themselves considering the client's request that the therapeutic relationship change to a friendship post therapy

The above-mentioned list of professional competencies are by no means exhaustive and we wish to repeat that they are published in order to stimulate critical reflection in training organizations, and within UKAPI and EAIP, in order to further develop the theory and practice of integrative psychotherapy.

12 Professional practice issues

In the last 20 or so years the professions of counselling and psychotherapy have grown dramatically, as evidenced in the growing number of practitioners and training programmes provided in the private sector and in higher education. Despite 100 years or so of psychotherapy we appear a very young profession, arguably still in its adolescence.

In this concluding chapter we take the opportunity to pause and give voice to some concerns which, in conversations with colleagues throughout the United Kingdom and Europe, we believe are shared by many in the field. In doing so our intention is to raise the issues. We do not pretend to have the answers. We wish to explore four particular areas of concern and acknowledge that the list could be considerably extended to. While both authors are members and/or officers of several professional organizations, the views expressed are our own and do not necessarily represent those of the organizations to which we belong or in which we hold office.

- Statutory regulation
- The politics of the therapy room
- Oppressive practice
- Challenges to training organizations

Statutory regulation

It has been over 30 years since the Foster Report recommended the regulation of psychotherapy in the United Kingdom. Partly in response to this report the United Kingdom Council for Psychotherapy (UKCP) was established in 1993 and launched the National Register of Psychotherapists at the House of Lords in the same year. The UKCP is an Incorporated Charitable

Company whose major objective is the protection of the public. This means that its 5,000 plus registrants must adhere to UKCP standards of training and ethical and professional practice. Annual randomized audits of the National Register have been introduced to ensure the high degree of accountability required of its members. Thus the UKCP has gone a long way to ensure 'that as high standards of self regulation as possible are adopted by UKCP member organizations and their practitioners, in the public interest' (Enever, 2003, Foreword to 10th edn).

However, the UKCP has not yet been able to deliver on its major goal of statutory regulation of the profession which remains '… an ideal towards which we are working' (Enever, 2003, Foreword). While UKCP has undoubtedly achieved significant influence and prestige in the United Kingdom and among leading European professional organizations, the failure to achieve statutory regulation is a massive 'unfinished agenda' with considerable consequences for many practitioners in the field.

We welcomed and actively engaged with the attempt of Lord Alderdyce to effect regulation through a Private Members' Bill, but this ultimately failed partly due to a lack of political will on the part of both houses of parliament (there being far more pressing concerns) but also because those psychotherapists who participated in the Working Party, and the organizations they represented, could not agree on certain fundamental issues. Regrettably suspicion among and between the representative groups party to the deliberations raised questions of credibility, in terms of which approaches should be acknowledged as a legitimate form of psychotherapy. In short which of the groups around the table, were considered to be 'in or out'? These deliberations further excluded many approaches and organizations that were unable to even get participation in the Working Party. A number of factors appear to us to be significant in creating this impasse.

Dogma

In our combined experience of over 60 years in the profession, it is possible to detect in most schools of psychotherapy those who tend towards fundamentalism and promote the purity of their approach, together with an explicit or implicit attitude of superiority over other approaches. Like all fundamentalists they have a tendency to irrational and arrogant behaviour, notably towards those within the same modality who do not aspire to purity, as well as those of other modalities who are clearly viewed as 'misguided'!

Indeed this phenomenon together with an alleged 480 plus schools of psychotherapy has led to comparisons of the profession with religion, each school presenting as a denomination with a claim to, even monopoly of, the 'truth'. Organizations like UKCP and the European Association for Psychotherapy (EAP) are a determined attempts to provide a structure in which the broad range of approaches can mutually co-exist and engage in collaborative work for the benefit of the public rather than the promulgation of the 'gospel' according to Freud, Jung, Rogers, Reich, Perls, Assagioli and so on. While both organizations are still developing and are ambitious projects, they each represent a considerable move towards a more ecumenical and mature profession.

Power

The issue of power, or rather the misuse of power is apparent to many in the field who find it near impossible to gain access to employment as a psychotherapist in the public sector, despite appropriate training. Two modalities of psychotherapy dominate the National Health Service in the United Kingdom, psychoanalytical psychotherapy and cognitive behavioural therapy. Whether the defence of the status quo is based on dogma or so-called evidenced based research, or officially denied, the reality is that the vast majority of modalities are being excluded. There are exceptions in certain areas of the country where other modalities are represented but their overall number is small, especially in relation to the number of alternative modalities. The majority of the public who rely on the National Health Service, often because of financial constraints, do not therefore have access to alternative modalities that are enjoyed by those who can afford to use the private sector.

Statutory regulation would likely lead to the creation of a psychotherapist grade within the NHS that, as an equal opportunities employer, should lead to greater opportunity for employment for those trained in alternative modalities and greater transparency of opportunity. Currently highly trained psychotherapists whose base profession is, for example nursing, are employed as Nurse Specialist Therapists or some such title and paid accordingly! In the highly competitive market place one has to ask the question to what extent market forces are influencing the debate on statutory regulation and whether the current psychotherapy market in the NHS, as described earlier, amounts to a monopoly and restrictive practice?

Lack of resources

Despite recommendations supporting a nationwide psychotherapy service in the NHS there seems little prospect of this happening in the foreseeable future, due largely to lack of resources. Indeed one has to ask whether such a service would be possible since it would require many more therapists that are presently available, unless there is an end to the discreet restrictive practice suggested earlier. Perhaps the issue of resources needed to fund such a service is another factor mitigating against statutory regulation as this may 'open the flood gates' and let in hordes of psychotherapists from other modalities?

In our opinion the factors determining the eligibility of any psychotherapy for regulation, traditional or contemporary, should depend not on dogma or restrictive practice, but on the existence of all of the following:

1. the level and sophistication of its training standards
2. the efficacy of its ethical and professional codes
3. the organizational infrastructure to effectively monitor the above, and
4. the range and depth of supporting literature and research

On the basis of these criteria the wide range of modalities represented in the UKCP and the EAP would successfully achieve statutory regulation and help further access to psychotherapy for the benefit of the wider public.

The politics of the therapy room

We have included earlier in this work a focus on the world of the client outside of the therapy room and particularly on the cultural, ecological and transpersonal dimensions that influence our clients day to day. An outstanding question that arises is whether a focus on such areas takes the psychotherapist into the realm of the political, since many issues raised in the multicultural and ecological domains especially involve political considerations? We conclude that this is inevitable since to ignore these issues in the client's life is a profound failure of empathy. It is also, perhaps unwittingly, a discreet and implicit political stance to the extent that in so doing the psychotherapist inevitably supports the status quo, which may be detrimental to the client's well-being? We believe that an awareness of the wider context in which we practice is more and more becoming the material of psychotherapy. This leads us into our next concern, oppressive practice in psychotherapy.

Oppressive practice

Research conducted by Thompson some ten years ago revealed that among four training courses in supervision there was little or no teaching on cultural issues (Thompson, 1991). In a recent publication we wrote of our more recent experience of psychotherapy trainees, with a social science or psychology background, having a greater awareness of the significance of cultural pluralism, concerned about the gross underrepresentation of members of ethnic minorities in psychotherapy training and demanding training courses to attend to issues of oppressive practice (Gilbert and Evans, 2000).

We believe that ignorance is a key factor in the perpetuation of oppressive practice in psychotherapy, supported by a complacency that comes from psychotherapists occupying a privileged position in society. Monotheoretical training programmes can tend to present their psychotherapy model as a rather self-contained body of knowledge, conveying the impression that a particular school represents the 'truth' of psychotherapy. Given that there are allegedly 480 schools of psychotherapy does this mean there are 480 'truths'? (Karuso, 1984). We agree with Espin and Gawalek, 'Theories of ... psychopathology have been notorious for their neglect of cultural variability as well as gender issues. Most psychological theory is literally Anglo-Saxon in its perspectives and conception of human nature' (1992, p. 88).

According to Ridley the medical model remains the dominant framework used by mental health professionals to understand and treat psychiatric problems, shared also by classical psychoanalysis which he claims is 'unsurpassed in shaping the thinking and practice of mental health treatment' (Ridley, 1995, p. 44). He goes on to argue that the medical model leads to unintentional racism through the tendency to reduce all social problems to intrapsychic processes, the tendency to over pathologize individuals and the consequent neglect of social, economic and political factors. In a similar vein Smail (1998) writes that the social structures that perpetuate oppressive practice represent the tyranny of normality. We offer these as questions for debate.

Our integrative model adopts an I–Thou attitude to the client, including the client's perception of their world outside the therapy room. We agree with Eleftheriadou who argues for a transcultural approach where the therapist is willing to engage with cultural difference seeking to appreciate the cultural influences on the client and co-creating a therapy relationship that aspires towards equality. This requires working with an attitude of horizontalization and attempting to avoid hierarchies in descriptions of behaviour (Eleftheriadou, 1994). It also requires that therapists examine their own world view and value system and critically reflect on how such may influence the therapeutic work.

Challenges to training organizations

In the first chapter on philosophy we raised issues of dogma in psychotherapy training organizations with regard to the creation of a culture of deference towards their psychotherapy model. In the section on oppressive practice we raised issues to do with the perpetuation of uncritical attitudes towards monotheoretical and culturally encapsulated theories. In our opinion the six dimensions of therapy that we explored earlier support the notion of the psychotherapist as 'reflexive practitioner' and we maintain that there is an educational and professional obligation on training organizations to model good practice by developing a culture of critical reflection in clinical practice by exploring self, the client and the process between. Such critical reflection needs to include a critique of the theoretical model and an exploration and evaluation of the philosophies and value systems underpinning the model and an exploration of issues of oppressive practice.

Developing 'a research mindset' can significantly enhance a trainee's capacity for critical reflection and we support the UKCP requirement to include a research component in psychotherapy training programmes. This still remains as a challenge for many training organizations. At best, programmes appear to include a lecture or two or a short module on research methods although some trainings have taken up the challenge to embed research findings into their ongoing teaching on such diverse subjects such as child development, neurobiology, psychopathology and trauma.

We frequently hear psychotherapists complain about research that challenges the efficacy of one or more aspects of clinical practice or indeed questions the value of psychotherapy itself. Surely psychotherapists themselves should be engaged in utilizing existing methods and developing new methods of research and thereby take the lead in evaluating the profession? Marvin Goldfried has long been a proponent of opening up the communication between psychotherapists and researchers so that research findings become more clinically applicable (Goldfried and Wolfe, 1996). We believe every psychotherapy training organization could take very seriously the idea of promoting this dialogue by encouraging clinicians to collaborate with researchers in an effort to generate clinically relevant findings. This would enable the trainees to become sensitive to the relevance of research for their clinical practice and in time engage in research themselves. We look forward to a time when collaborative research projects involving a group of trainees may be embedded in the curriculum. It is even possible for training organizations to consider collaborating with others to pool resources.

In recent years we have heard several trainers express concern about the duration of training (currently a minimum of four years) which they consider too short. Some trainers believe it takes at least seven years to really assimilate the theory and practice. While sympathetic to this viewpoint it is difficult to ascertain with any real accuracy if the appropriate length of training would be seven years? Nine years? Or longer? The problem of determining the duration of therapy training is partly that some people take longer than others to assimilate the appropriate degree of knowledge and skill. However, the lack of a set of core competencies across the profession has made it difficult to ascertain with any real confidence just what knowledge and skills need to be assessed. Currently, it is often a 'hit and miss' affair dependent either on the subjective assessment of the trainer(s) which can be problematic. Some institutions combine a written case study submission with a viva examination. Arguably not all people perform equally well in viva examinations and perhaps in time, different combinations of assessment processes will be employed when we have agreed core competencies and how to assess these most effectively. In 2000 the UKCP voted in a set of generic competencies with an overwhelming majority in support. Subsequently, each modality will eventually further develop a set of competencies specific to their approach, perhaps in a similar format to the ones we developed in Chapter 11? While these set of competencies for integrative psychotherapy remain 'a work in progress' when completed we will more accurately know what it is we are evaluating.

We suggest rather that it would be wise to acknowledge the economic constraints of stretching training beyond that which is affordable. Indeed many would argue this is already the case and that the cost of training puts the profession beyond the reach of many, thereby inadvertently discriminating against those on lower incomes?

We assume development as a psychotherapist continues throughout one's career, as suggested by the insistence by UKCP, and most all other professional bodies, on continuing professional development as an ethical requirement. In his book *Wisdom in the Practice of Psychotherapy* Karuso's thoughts about the process of long-term therapy apply equally well to the process of psychotherapy training 'it is a slow cooking process for which there is no microwave substitute' (Karuso, quoted in Dryden and Norcross, 1990).

We wonder whether it is time to consider the introduction of a seniority grade into the field, whereby a practitioner can be confirmed by his professional organization as a senior psychotherapist after a certain level of experience and evaluation, and perhaps then at consultant level, much the same as in the medical and allied professions? This would encourage experienced therapists to consider remaining in the field rather than seeking managerial or training positions. Perhaps this could be linked with one's growth and development as a supervisor? We think this would encourage the notion that learning is indeed lifelong and give more impetus to post-qualification training and professional development.

We have also discussed with many trainers concerns about the entry requirements, or rather the apparent inflexibility of the requirements for entry to the profession. The UKCP have, rightly in our opinion, established entry to psychotherapy training at postgraduate level and the training at a level equivalent to a Master's degree. However, the UKCP does honour prior training for equivalence and relevant life experience at entry level. A number of UKCP training programmes delivered in member training organizations are also validated by a university for the award of MA or MSc. Both authors have designed and ran university validated courses in psychotherapy.

However, we are sympathetic to those who are concerned that there may be potential applicants who are put off from making application by the lack of a first degree or equivalent. One of the positive advantages of university validation is that higher education has developed some effective methods for accrediting prior certificated learning and prior experiential learning that can be relatively easily adapted to encourage wider access to psychotherapy programmes. One of the authors has also experimented with taking a small number of applicants with little academic background into the first year of training under a period of 'probation' with continued training dependent on achieving successful completion of the first year. Usually this has entailed a trainee arranging tuition at a local college or privately to develop their writing skills. Significantly not one of the several trainees who entered the programme in this way over a number of years failed to successfully complete their training and register as a psychotherapist. A senior colleague at a local university, that takes seriously the notion of lifelong learning, confirmed that, in his experience, older students who enter university with minimal certification consistently perform better than younger students with higher entry certification. He believed this was largely a matter of personal motivation than academic ability.

An ongoing concern expressed by trainers, training organizations and trainees, especially on university validated programmes, has been the constant need to balance the academic demands of the university with the clinical demands of the profession. We know of no trainers who claim to always achieve the correct balance. Perhaps it is time to create a support organization for trainers? Most organizations have to juggle with the demand for improved resources whilst not pricing themselves out of the market. Perhaps it is time to create a support organization for directors and managers of training organizations?

Trainees are required to attend to their own personal therapy, achieve the required number of clinical hours with clients, meet the requirements for clinical supervision, complete a mental health placement, and in some organizations a further requirement to attend professional conferences. In addition there is attendance at workshops and lectures, reading, completion of written submissions – essays, case studies, research projects and so on. One cannot suspend life with all its demands and opportunities while engaging in psychotherapy education! Maintaining a healthy balance between home, work and training is highly challenging and we are very appreciative and inspired by the level of commitment of those who choose to put themselves through this demanding process. Perhaps it is time for trainees to create a trade union?

Appendix: Analysis of contact functions (based on original from Gilles Delisle)

A. How does Phillip seem to use his contact functions?

1. Eyes, seeing

1a   During what kind of interaction does Phillip look at me?
When asking a question ...

1b   During what sort of interaction does Phillip avoid me?
When suppressing physical sensation and emotion ...

1c   Description of the eyes and his way of seeing (large, small, arched eyebrows, bulging etc).
Looks intently when making fleeting eye contact ...

1d   What emotions do the eyes seem to express?
Anxiety, fear, anger, sadness.

1e   What do I feel in terms of these eyes and this way of looking?
Irritation in response to his scrutinizing stare. Warmth in response to his sadness.

Impressionist assessment of 'seeing contact function'. (1 low; 5 high)

1   (2)   3   4   5

2. Voice, speech

2a Description of the voice (hoarse, strong, sing-song, soft?)
Strong, slightly wingeing.

2b What emotions does the voice seem to express?
Predominantly anger and resentment; hidden fear and sadness.

2c What do I feel in terms of this voice?
Anger in response to his resentment. Warmth and concern in response to his fear.

2d Does the individual use it in a clear and precise way or is it filled with generalizations. Does it ask questions? Etc.
Generalized discounting remarks about colleagues and family members.

2e What do I feel in terms of these words?
Anxiety and irritation in response to a sense of being interrogated. Warmth and compassion in response to his underlying anxiety and sadness.

Impressionist assessment of the 'voice; speech' contact function. (1 low; 5 high)

1   ②   3   4   5

3. Hearing

3a Does Phillip seem to hear me easily? Does he make me repeat my questions and comments?
My input is economical because Phillip dominates the session verbally. He appears to hear me easily.

3b Does he hear something other than what I say?
He appears attuned to anticipated criticism.

3c Do I have the feeling that it's easy for me to be heard by Phillip, and to be understood?
He hears but does not understand communication regarding emotions.

Impressionist assessmant of the 'hearing' contact function. (1 low; 5 high)

1   (2)   3   4   5

4. Touch, movement, appearance

4a How does Phillip present himself visually?
Does his presentation seem consistent or inconsistent with what
he says?
*Neat and casual clothing, well groomed and precise to the point of
being self-conscious about his appearance.*

4b Does he touch me? What do I feel when he touches me? Do I
want to touch him? When? How?
*Phillip makes no attempt to shake my hand, and I do not wish him
to because of smouldering anger he emits.*
*I feel repulsed by the possibility of physical contact, particularly his
smouldering anger.*

4c How does Phillip use his body in relation to space? (Does he
seem to fill up the space; gaze through it; disappear it?)
*He walks quickly and sits with arms folded across his chest and legs
crossed. I intuit an invisible sign reading 'Keep your distance'.*

Impressionist assessment of the 'touch, movement, appearance'
contact function. (1 low; 5 high)

①   2   3   4   5

B. How does Phillip use his support functions?

1. Daily support

1a How does Phillip say that he supports himself during periods of excitement or difficulty (social networks, alcohol, drugs, drinking, recreational pursuits, sleep, respiration?) Self reliant and autonomous.

1b How would I place hime in a support continuum in general? Self sufficiency (a)✓ _____(z) Environmental support.

2. Support during interview

2a How does the person breathe at different moments of the interview?
Phillip's breathing is shallow and appears to 'cease' when struggling to suppress feelings.

2b How does he sit?
Legs crossed; arms folded across his chest.

2c Any other observations on the subject of support (also contact functions in a support perspective).
None.

2d Do I feel that I have to be tactful or reassuring with Phillip?
I feel I need to be cautious and tactful.

2e How does he react in a situation of slight anxiety? (example, in moments of silence or when *I present a blank expression*)
Tight jaw; clenched fists; rigid body; critical of others.

2f Where would I place him on a support continuum during an interview?
Self sufficiency (a)✓ _____(z) Therapist's support.

2g Are there any links between the way in which he claims to support himself and the way in which he manages his support during an interview.
Both in the session and in his life in general, Phillip impresses as highly self-sufficient and deeply anxious about receiving external support.

C. How does dysfunction manifest itself in the awareness cycle?

1 Does he seem fixed on a particular point?
   Appears highly immobilized (see A below); suppresses his energy, witholds emotional expression except for resentment and anger.

2 Are there points which seem to disturb him? (action, contact, withdrwawal etc.)
   Sensation (see B below) Phillip appears physically uncomfortable when suppressing.

3 Do I recognize something that has occurred in the interview in terms of his reason for the referral? Can I place it within awareness?
   Incongruity between his emotional illiteracy and apparent neediness (unconscious) and his reason for at tending therapy (job prospects) therefore blocked at awareness (see C below).

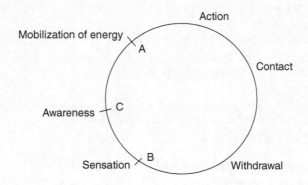

D. How will dysfunction be maintained?

1 How does he resist during an interview? (confluence, introjection, projection, retroflection, deflection?)
Desensitises physicality-A.
Retroflects energy and emotion-B.
Introjection blocks awareness-C.

2 Does he seem capable of resisting with awareness? (i.e. chooses to not look at me; doesn't wish to respond and says so, etc.)
No.

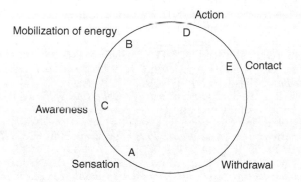

A = desensitisation
B = retroflection
C = introjection
D = He further projects criticism on to the therapist
E = He deflects and thereby minimizes contact with therapist

Bibliography

Arkowitz, A. (2002) 'Toward an Integrative Perspective on Resistance to Change, in Resistance to Change in Psychotherapy', *Journal of Clinical Psychology*, 58 (2).

Aron, L. (1998) 'The Clinical Body and the Reflexive Mind', in *Relational Perspectives on the Body*, L. Aron and F. Sommer-Anderson (eds). Hillsdale, NJ: The Analytic Press.

Aron, L. (1999) 'The Patient's Experience of the Analyst's Subjectivity', in *Relational Psychoanalysis*, Stephen A. Mitchell and L. Aron (eds). Hillsdale, NJ: The Analytic Press.

Aron, L. E. and Sommer-Anderson, F. (1998) *Relational Perspectives on the Body*. Hillsdale, NJ: The Analytic Press.

Assagioli, R. (1965) *Psychosynthesis: A Collection of Basic Writings*. New York: Viking Compass.

Atwood, G. E. and Stolorow, R. D. (1984) *Structures of Subjectivity: Explorations in Psychoanalytic Phenomenology*. Hillsdale, NJ: The Analytic Press.

Barton, A. (1974) *Three Worlds of Therapy: An Existential – Phenomenological Study of Therapies of Freud Jung and Rogers*. Palo Alto, CA: Mayfield.

Beebe, B. and Lachmann, F. M. (1998) 'Co-constructing Inner Relational Processes', *Psychoanalytic Psychology*, 15 (4), pp. 480–516.

Beisser, A. R. (1970) 'The Paradoxical Theory of Changes', in *Gestalt Therapy Now*, J. Sagan and I. Shepherd (eds). Palo Alto, CA: Science and Behaviour Books.

Bernard, J. M. (1994) 'Ethical and Legal Dimensions of Supervision', in *Supervision: Exploring the Effective Components*, L. D. Borders (ed.). ERIC/CUSS Digest Series. Greensboro, NC: University of North Carolina.

Berne, E. (1961) *Transactional Analysis in Psychotherapy*. New York: Ballantine Books.

Berne, E. (1974) *What Do You Say After You Say Hello?* London: Corgi Books.

Bernstein, R. J. (1992) *The New Constellation: The Ethical-Political Horizons Of Modernity, Postmodernity*. Cambridge, MA: MIT Press.

Black, T. and Holford, L. (eds) (1999) *Introducing Qualitative Research: A Distance Learning Study Guide*. Guildford: School of Educational Studies, University of Surrey.

Bohart, A. C. (2000) 'The Client is the Most Important Common Factor: Clients' Self-Healing Capacities and Psychotherapy', *Journal of Psychotherapy Integration*, 10 (2), pp. 127–49.

Bowlby, J. (1988) *A Secure Base: Clinical Applications of Attachment Theory*. London: Routledge.

Bollas, C. (1991) *The Shadow of the Object*. London: Free Association Books.

Borders, L. D. (ed.) *Supervision: Exploring the Effective Components*. ERIC/CUSS Digest Series. Greensboro, NC: University of North Carolina.

Bordin, E. S. (1979) 'The Generalisability of the Psychoanalytic Concept of the Working Alliance', *Psychotherapy* 16, pp. 252–60.

Bovasso, G. B., Williams, W. E. and Haroutune, K. A. (1999) 'The Long-term Outcomes of Mental Health Treatment in a Population-Based Study', *Journal of Consulting and Clinical Psychology*, 67 (4), pp. 529–38.

Buber, M. (1923, 1996) *I and Thou*. Translated by Kaufman, New York: Touchstone.

Carroll, M. (1996) *Counselling Supervision, Theory Skills and Practice*. London: Cozily.

Cashdan, S. (1988) *Object Relations Therapy: Using the Relationship*. New York: W.W. Norton & Co.

Casement, P. (1985) *On Learning from the Patient*. London: Routledge.

Chaudhuri, H. (1975) 'Psychology: Humanistic and Transpersonal', *Journal of Humanistic Psychology*, 15 (1), p. 8.

Clarkson, P. (1989) *Gestalt Counselling in Action* (2nd edition). London: Sage.

Clarkson, P. (1990) 'A Multiplicity of Psychotherapeutic Relationships', *British Journal of Psychotherapy*, 7 (2), pp. 148 63.

Clarkson, P. (1992) *Transactional Analysis Psychotherapy*. London: Routledge.

Clarkson, P. and Lapworth, P. (1992) 'Systemic Integrative Psychotherapy', in *Integrative and Eclectic Therapy: A Handbook*, Windy Dryden (ed.). Bucks: Open University Press.

Clarkson, P. and Mackewn, J. (1993) *Fritz Perls*. London: Sage.

Clemmens, M. C. and Bursztyn, A. (2003) 'Culture and Body: A Phenomenological and Dialogic Inquiry', *British Gestalt Journal*, 12 (1), pp. 15–21.

Cohen, L. and Manion, L. (1994) *Research Methods in Education* (4th edition). London: Routledge.

Cooper, S. H. (2000) *Objects of Hope*. Hillsdale, NJ: The Analytic Press.

Cushman, P. (1995) *Constructing The Self, Constructing America: A Cultural History of Psychotherapy*. New York: Addison-Wesley.

De Lise, G. (1991) 'A Gestalt Perspective of Personality Disorders', *The British Gestalt Journal*, 1 (1), pp. 42–50.

Denzin, N. K. and Lincoln, Y. S. (eds) (2000) 'Introduction: The Discipline and Practice of Qualitative Research', in *Handbook of Qualitative Research* (2nd edition). Thousand Oaks, CA: Sage.

DeYoung, P. (2003) *Relational Psychotherapy: A Primer.* New York: Brunner-Routledge.
Doehrman, M. J. (1976) 'Parallel Process in Supervision and Psychotherapy', *Bulletin of the Menninger Clinic*, 40 (1), pp. 1–104.
Dollard, J. and Miller, N. E. (1950) *Personality and Psychotherapy.* New York: McGraw-Hill.
Downing, J. N. (2000) *Between Conviction and Uncertainty. Philosophical Guidelines for the Practicing Psychotherapist.* New York: State University of New York Press.
Dryden, W. and Norcross, J. C. (1990) *Eclecticism in Counselling and Psychotherapy.* Ipswich: Gale Centre Publications.
Ekstein, R. and Wallerstein, R. S. (1972) *The Teaching and Learning of Psychotherapy.* New York: International Universities Press.
Eleftheriadou, Z. (1994) *Transcultural Counselling.* London: Central Book Publishing.
Enever, A. (2003) *The National Register of Psychotherapists* (10th Anniversary edition). UKCP/ London: Brunner-Routledge.
Epstein, M. (1996) *Thoughts Without a Thinker.* Psychotherapy from a Buddhist Perspective. New York: Basic Books. Perseus Books Group (Publication Date 31/01/2005).
Erskine, R. G. and Trautmann, R. L. (1996) 'Methods of Integrative Psychotherapy', *Transactional Analysis Journal*, 26 (4), pp. 318–28.
Espin, O. and Gawalek, K. (1992) 'Women's Diversity, Ethnicity, Race, Class and Gender Theories of Feminist Psychology', in *Personality and Pathology*, L. S. Brown and M. Ballot (eds). New York: Guildford Press.
Evans, K. R. (1994a) 'Shame – A Gestalt Perspective', *Transactional Analysis Journal* 24 (2).
Evans, K. R. (1994b) A Review of 'Diagnosis: The Struggle for a Meaningful Paradigm', in *Gestalt Therapy: Perspectives and Applications*, J. Melnick and S. M. Nevis (1992). New York Gestalt Institute of Cleveland, Gardner Press, *British Gestalt Journal*, 1994, 3 (1).
Evans, K. (1996) 'True Dialogue Requires an Appreciation of Difference', *International Journal of Psychotherapy*, 1 (1), pp. 91–3.
Evans, K. (1999) 'An Integrative Approach to Assessment and Diagnosis', *Australian Gestalt Journal*, 2 (2).
Ferenczi, S. (1988) *The Clinical Diary of Sandor Ferenczi.* Edited by Judith Dupont. Translated by Michael Balint and Nicola Zarday Jackson. Massachusetts: Harvard University Press.
Fiedler, F. E. (1950) 'A Comparison of Therapeutic Relationships in Psychoanalytic, Nondirective and Adlerian Therapy', *Journal of Consulting Psychology*, 14, pp. 239–45.
Fishman, D. B. (1999) *The Case for Ongoing Pragmatic Psychology.* New York: New York University Press.
Fonaghy, P., Gergely, G., Jurist, E. L. and Target, M. (2002) *Affect Regulation, Mentalization, and the Development of the Self.* New York: Other Press.
Frank, J. D. (1982) 'Therapeutic Components Shared by all Psychotherapies', in *Psychotherapy Research and Behaviour Change*,

J. H. Harvey and M. M. Peeks (eds). Washington, DC: American Psychological Association, pp. 9–37.

Frank, J. D. and Frank, J. B. (1991) *Persuasion and Healing: A Comparative Study of Psychotherapy* (3rd edition). Baltimore, MD: John Hopkins University Press.

Frankl, V. (1966) 'Self-transcendence as a Human Phenomenon', *Journal of Humanistic Psychology*, 6, Fall.

French, T. M. (1933) 'Interrelations Between Psychoanalysis and the Experimental Work of Pavlov', *American Journal of Psychiatry*, 89, pp. 1165–203.

Freud, Sophie (2002) 'Jung and Freud – False Prophets', A lecture at Freuds Bar, Sodra Teatern/Kagelbanan, Stockholm, Sweden.

Friedman, M. (2002) 'Martin Buber and Dialogical Psychotherapy', *Journal of Humanistic Psychology*, 42 (4), Fall, pp. 7–36.

Francis, A. J. (1987) 'DSM-11R Personality Disorders: Diagnosis and Treatment', B.M.A. Audio Cassettes. New York: Guildford Press.

Gergen, K. J. (1992) 'Towards a Postmodern Psychology', in *Psychology and Postmodernism: Inquiries in Social Construction*, S. Kvale (ed.). London: Sage.

Gerson, S. (2004) 'The Relational Unconscious: A Core Element of Intersubjectivity, Thirdness and Clinical Process', *Psychoanalytic Quarterly*, LXXIII.

Gilbert, M. and Evans, K. (2000) *Psychotherapy Supervision. An Integrative Relational Approach*. Buckingham: Open University Press.

Goldfried, M. R. (1995a) *From Cognitive-Behavior Therapy to Psychotherapy Integration*. New York: Springer Publishing Company.

Goldfried, M. R. (1995b) 'Toward a Common Language for Case Formulation', *Journal for Psychotherapy Integration*, 5 (3), pp. 221–4.

Goldfried, M. R. and Wolfe, B. E. (1996) 'Psychotherapy Practice and Research: Repairing a Strained Alliance', *American Psychologist*, October, pp. 1007–16.

Greenberg, L. S., Rice, L. N. and Elliott, R. (1988) *Facilitating Emotional Change: The Moment-by-Moment Process*. New York: Guildford Press.

Guy, J. D. and Brady, J. L. (2001) 'Identifying the Faces in the Mirror: Untangling Transference and Countertransference in Self Psychology', *Journal of Clinical Psychology*, 57 (8), pp. 993–7.

Hargaden, H. and Sills, C. (2002) *Transactional Analysis: A Relational Perspective*. UK: Brunner-Routledge.

Hawkins, P. and Shohet, R. (2000) *Supervision in the Helping Professions* (2nd edition). Buckingham: Open University Press.

Heath, G. (2000) 'A Constructivist Attempts to Talk to the Field', *International Journal of Psychotherapy*, 5 (1), pp. 11–35. European Association of Psychotherapy.

Holland, L. A. (2000) *Philosophy for Counselling and Psychotherapy*. London: Macmillan Press.

Holmes, J. (1993) *John Bowlby and Attachment Theory*. New York: Routledge.

Howard, G. (1997) *Ecological Psychology: Creating a more Earth Friendly Human Nature*. Notre Dame, IN: University of Notre Dame.

Hubble, M. A., Duncan, B. L. and Scott, D. M. (2000) *The Heart and Soul of Change*. Washington, DC: APA.

Hycner, R. (1991) *Between Person and Person*. New York: The Gestalt Journal Press.

Hycner, R. and Jacobs, L. (1995) *The Healing Relationship*. New York: The Gestalt Journal Press.

Jacobs, L. (1989) 'Dialogue in Gestalt Theory and Therapy', *Gestalt Journal*, 12 (1), pp. 25–68.

Karuso, quoted in Dryden, W. and Norcross, J. (1990) *Eclectism and Integration in Counselling and Psychotherapy*. Ipswich: Gale Centre Publications.

Kiesler, D. J. (1988) *Therapeutic Metacommunication: Therapist Impact Disclosure as Feedback in Psychotherapy*. Palo Alto, CA: Consulting Psychologists Press.

Kiesler, D. J. (1996) *Contemporary Interpersonal Theory and Research: Personality, Psychopathology, and Psychotherapy*. New York: Wiley.

Kelly, G. A. (1955) *The Psychology of Personal Constructs*. New York: W.W. Norton & Co.

King, Y. (1990) 'Healing the Wounds: Feminism, Ecology and the Nature Culture Dualism', in *Reweaving the World: The Emergence of Eco-feminism*, Diamond and G. F. Orenstein (eds). San Francisco, CA: Sierra Club Books, pp. 106–21.

Kohut, H. (1977) *The Restoration of the Self*. New York: International Universities Press.

Kohut, H. (1978) *The Search for the Self: Volume 2*, Paul Ornstein (ed.). New York: International Universities Press.

Kohut, H. (1984) *How Does Analysis Cure?* A. Goldberg and P. Stepansky (eds). Chicago, IL: University of Chicago Press.

Korb, M. P., Gorrell, J. and Van De Riet, V. (1989) *Gestalt Therapy, Practice and Theory*. Boston, MA: Allyn & Bacon.

Krause, I. (1998) *Therapy Across Culture*. London: Sage.

Krueger, D. W. (1989) *Body Self Psychological Self*. New York: Brunner/Mazel.

Kuhn, J. L. (2001) 'Towards an Ecological Humanistic Psychology', *Journal of Humanistic Psychology*, 41 (2), Spring.

Kuhn, T. S. (1962) *The Structure of Scientific Revolutions*. Chicago, IL: University of Chicago Press.

Kvale, S. (1992) *Psychology and Modernism*. London: Sage.

Lambert, M. J. and Arnold, R. C. (1987) 'Research and the Supervisary Process', *Professional Psychology: Research and Practice* (USA), 18 (3), pp. 217–24.

Langs, R. (1994) *Doing Supervision and Being Supervised*. London: Karnac Books.

Lasch, C. (1979) *The Culture of Narcissism*. New York: W.W. Norton & Co.

Lawson, H. (2001) *Closure, A Story of Everything*. London: Routledge.

Lazarus, A. A. (1981) *The Practice of Multi-Modal Therapy*. New York: McGraw Hill.

Lewin, K. (1952) *Field Theory in Social Science*. London: Tavistock.

Linehan, M. L. (1993) *Cognitive-Behavioral Treatment for Borderline Personality Disorder*. New York: Guilford Press.

Loewenthal, D. (1996) 'The Post-modern Counsellor: Some Implications for Practice, Theory, Research and Professionalism', *Counselling Psychology Quarterly*, 8 (4), pp. 373–81.

Lowe, R. (1999) 'Between the "No Longer" and the "Not Yet": Postmodernism as a Context for Critical Therapeutic Work', in *Deconstructing Psychotherapy*, I. Parker (ed.). London: Sage.

Luborsky, L., Singer, B. and Luborsky, L. (1975) 'Comparative Studies of Psychotherapy: Is it True that Eveyone has Won and all Will have Prizes?', *Archives of Ageneral Psychiatry*, 32, pp. 995–1008.

Lyotard Jean Francois (1996) *The Postmodern Condition: A Report on Knowledge*. Manchester: Manchester University Press.

Mace, C. (1999) 'Introduction: Philosophy and Psychotherapy', in *Heart and Soul: The Therapeutic Face of Philosophy*, C. Mace (ed.). London: Routledge.

Mackewn, J. (1997) *Developing Gestalt Counselling*. London: Sage.

Mahoney, M. J. (1991) *Human Change Processes: The Scientific Foundations of Psychotherapy*. New York: Basic Books.

Mahrer, A. R. (1989) *The Integration of Psychotherapies*. New York: Plenum Publishing.

Maroda, K. J. (1991) *The Power of the Countertransference*. New York: Jason Aronson.

Maslow, A. (1968) *Toward a Psychology of Being* (2nd edition). New York: Van Nostrand Reinhold, pp. iii–v.

May, R. (1985) *The Third Humanism*. AHP Perspective. CA: AHP.

Melnick, J. and Nevis, S. M. (1992) *Gestalt Therapy: Perspectives and Applications*. New York: Gestalt Institute of Cleveland, Gardner Press.

Messer, S. B. (2001) 'Introduction to the Special Issue on Assimilative Integration', *Journal of Psychotherapy Integration*, 11 (1).

Metzner, R. (1999) *Green Psychology: Transforming our Relationship to the Earth*. Rochester, VT: Park Street Books.

Millet, K. (1969) *Sexual Politics*. New York: Avon Books.

Mitchell, S. A. and Aron, L. (eds) (1999) *Relational Psychoanalysis*. Hillsdale, NJ: The Analytic Press.

Moustakas, C. (1985) 'Humanistic or Humanism?', *Journal of Humanistic Psychology*, 25 (3).

Moustakis, C. (1994) *Phenomenological Research Methods*. London: Sage.

Naess, A. (1989) *Ecology, Community and Lifestyle: Outline of an Ecosophy*. Cambridge, MA: Cambridge University Press.

Norcross, J. C. and Goldfried, M. R. (eds) (1992) *Handbook of Psychotherapy Integration*. New York: Basic Books.

Ogden, T. H. (1994) 'The Analytic Third: Working with Intersubjective Clinical facts', in *Relational Psychoanalysis*, S. A. Mitchell, and L. Aron (eds) (1999). Hillsdale, NJ: The Analytic Press.

Opazo, R. (1997) 'In the Hurricanes Eye: A Supraparadigmatic Integrative Model', *Journal of Psychotherapy Integration*, 7 (1), pp. 17–54.

Orange, D. (1995) *Emotional Understanding: Studies in Psychoanalytic Epistemology*. New York: Guildford Press.

Orbach, S. (2003) 'There is No Such Thing as a Body', *British Journal of Psychotherapy*, 20 (1), pp. 3–15.

Pannenberg, W. (1983) *Jesus: God and Man*. Westminster: John Knox Press.

Parlett, M. (1991) 'Reflections on Field Theory', *British Gestalt Journal*, 1 (2), pp. 69–81.

Paul, G. L. (1967) 'Strategy of Outcome Research in Psychotherapy', *Journal of Consulting Psychology*, 31 (2), pp. 109–18.

Pederson, B. P. (1997) *Culture Centred Counselling Interventions*. London: Sage.

Perls, F., Hefferline, R. and Goodman, P. (1951/94) 'Gestalt Therapy: Excitement and Growth in the Human Personality', *Gestalt Journal Press*, New York: Highland.

Polkinghorne, D. E. (1992) 'Postmodern Epistemology of Practice', in *Psychology and Postmodernism: Inquiries in Social Construction*, S. Kvale (ed.). London: Sage.

Polster, E. and Polster, M. (1974) *Gestalt Therapy Integrated: Contours of Theory and Practice*. New York: Vintage Books.

Polster, E. (1987) *Every Person's Life is Worth a Novel*. New York: W.W. Norton & Co.

Polster, E. (1995) *A Population of Selves*. San Francisco, CA: Jossey-Bass.

Pilisuk, M. (2001) 'Ecological Psychology and the Boundaries of the Person', *Journal Humanistic Psychology*, 41, Spring, Sage Publications.

Reason, P. (1994) *Participation in Human Inquiry*. London: Sage.

Ridley, C. R. (1995) *Overcoming Intentional Racism in Counseling and Therapy: A Practitioners Guide for Intentional Intervention*. London: Sage.

Rogers, C. R. (1951) *Client-centered Therapy*. Boston, MA: Houghton Mifflin.

Rosen, H. (1996) 'Meaning-Making Narratives: Foundations For Constructivist and Social Constructivist Psychotherapies', in *Constructing Realities: Meaning Making Perspectives for Psychotherapists: Inquiries in Social Construction*, H. Rosen and K. T. Kuehlwein (eds). London: Sage.

Roth, A. and Fonaghy, P. (1996) *What Works for Whom? A Critical Review of Psychotherapy Research.* New York: Guilford Press.

Rozak, T. (1992) *The Voice of the Earth: An Exploration of Ecopsychology.* New York: Simon & Schuster.

Ryle, A. (1990) *Cognitive-analytic Therapy: Active Participation in Change.* Chicester: John Wiley.

Samuels, A. (1993) *The Political Psyche.* London: Routledge.

Schore, A. W. (1994) *Affect Regulation and the Origin of the Self.* Hillsdale, NJ: The Analytic Press.

Searles, H. (1955) 'The Informational Value of the Supervisor's Emotional Experience' in *Collected Papers on Schizophrenia and Related Subjects,* H. Searles (1965). London: Hogarth Press.

Siegel, D. (1999) *The Developing Mind.* New York: Guildford Press.

Smail, D. (1988) *How to Survive without Psychotherapy.* London: Constable.

Smith, M. L. and Glass, C. V. (1977) 'Meta-analysis of Psychotherapy Outcome Studies', *American Psychologist,* 32, pp. 752–60.

Spotnitz, H. (1969) *Modern Psychoanalysis of the Schizophrenic Patient.* New York: Grune & Stratton.

Stern, D. N. (1985) *The Interpersonal World of the Infant.* New York: Basic Books.

Stolorow, R. D. and Atwood, G. E. (1992) *Contexts of Being.* Hillsdale, NJ: The Analytic Press.

Stoltenberg, C. D. and Delworth, U. (1986) *Supervising Counsellors and Therapists.* San Francisco, CA: Jossey-Bass.

Stricker, G. and Gold, J. R. (1996) 'Psychotherapy Integration: An Assimilative, Psychodynamic Approach', *Clinical Psychology: Science and Practice,* 3, pp. 47–58.

Tanesini, A. (1999) *An Introduction to Feminist Epistemologies.* Oxford: Blackwell.

Tansey, M. J. and Burke, W. F. (1989) *Understanding Counter-transference: From Projective Identification to Empathy.* Hillsdale, NJ: The Analytic Press.

Thompson, J. (1991) 'Issues of Race and Culture in Supervision Training Courses', MSc thesis, Polytechnic of East London.

Tobin, S. (1990) 'Self Psychology as a Bridge between Existential-Humanistic Psychology and Psychoanalysis', *Journal of Humanistic Psychology,* 30 (1), pp. 14–63.

Tolman, C. W. (1994) *Psychology, Society and Subjectivity.* London: Routledge.

Tolpin, M. (1997) 'Compensatory Structures: Paths to the Restoration of the Self', in *Conversations in Self Psychology: Progress in Self Psychology,* Volume 13, A. Goldberg (ed.). Hillsdale, NJ: The Analytic Press.

Trevarthen, C. (1998) 'Passionate Observers', video presentation in 'Baby Brains' Series. London: Tavistock Clinic.

Varela, E. S., Thompson, E. and Rosch, E. (1993) *The Embodied Mind: Cognitive Science and Human Experience.* London: MIT Press.

Wachtel, P. L. (1977) *Psychoanalysis and Behaviour Therapy: Toward an Integration*. New York: Basic Books.

Wampold, B. E., Mondin, G. W., Moody, M., Stich, F., Benson, K. and Hyun-nie Ahn (1997) 'A Meta-analysis of Outcome Studies Comparing Bona fide Psychotherapies. Empirically, all must have Prizes', *Psychological Bulletin*, 123, pp. 203–16.

Wampold, B. E. (2001) *The Great Psychotherapy Debate*. New Jersey: Lawrence Erlbaum Associates.

Wheeler, G. (1991) *Gestalt Reconsidered: A New Approach to Contact and Resistance*. New York: Gardner Press.

Wilber, K. (1980) *The Atman Project*. Illinois: Quest.

Winnicott, D. W. (1968) 'The Use of an Object and Relating Through Identifications' in *Psychoanalytic Explorations*, C. Winnicott, R. Shepherd and M. Davis (eds) (1989). London: Karnac Books.

Wolfe, B. E. and Goldfried, M. R. (1988) 'Research on Psychotherapy Integration and Conclusions from an NIMH Workshop', *Journal of Consulting and Clinical Psychology*, 56 (3), pp. 448–51.

Wolfe, B. E. (2001) 'A Message to Assimilative Integrationists: It's Time to Become Accommodative Integrationists: A Commentary', in *Journal of Psychotherapy Integration*, 11 (1), pp. 123–33.

Wright, K. (1991) *Vision and Separation: Between Mother and Baby*. London: Free Association Books.

Yalom, I. D. (1985) *The Theory and Practice of Group Psychotherapy*. New York: Basic Books.

Yalom, I. D. (1995) *The Theory and Practice of Group Psychotherapy* (4th edition). New York: Basic Books.

Yontef, G. M. (1988) 'Assimilating Diagnostic and Psychoanalytical Perspectives into Gestalt Therapy', *Gestalt Journal*, 11 (1), pp. 5–32.

Yontef, G. (2002) 'Relational Attitude in Gestalt Therapy', *International Gestalt Journal*, 25 (1), pp. 15–35.

Zinker, J. (1978) *Creative Process in Gestalt Therapy*. New York: Vintage Books.

Index

absolutism 14
adherence 38, 39
Alderdyce, Lord 158
allegiance 38–9
Arkowitz, A. 106
Arnold, R. C. 41
Aron, L. E. 48, 50, 51, 52, 54, 66, 67, 70, 72, 75, 78, 79
Assagioli, R. 56
assimilative integration 29–30
Atwood, G. E. 53, 65, 67, 77, 78, 79, 136

Bachelor, A. 41
Beck, A. 38
Beebe, B. 48, 76
behaviourism 21, 22, 24
   comic vision 22–3
behaviour therapy 22, 24, 31, 37
Bernard, J. M. 57
Berne, E. 53, 95
Bernstein, R. J. 14
Black, T. 13
Bohart, A. C. 40, 42
Bollas, C. 74, 135
Bordin, E. S. 36–7
Bovasso, G. B. 42
Bowlby, J. 61
Brady, J. L. 130
Brandchaft, B. 77
British Journal of Psychotherapy Integration, The 148
Buber, Martin 4, 17, 53, 71, 72, 76
Burke, W. F. 120, 121
Bursztyn, A. 48

Carroll, M. 134
case formulation
   common language for 8, 29
Casement, P. 133, 135

Cashdan, S. 136
Chaudhuri, H. 62
child development 72–3, 79, 99
   neurobiological basis of 32, 33
   see also mother–child relationship; parent–child relationship
Clarkson, P. 26, 73
Clemmens, M. C. 48
client–analyst relationship 2–3, 17–19, 32, 66–7, 69–70, 74–5, 76, 77–8, 150, 154
   case study 86–8, 118–20
   research 36–7, 40–1
client resistance 106, 110, 111
client safety 138, 139
co-creation of therapeutic relationship 2, 17–18, 32, 43, 65–6, 142
codetermination *see* co-creation
cognitive-analytic therapy 31
cognitive-behaviour therapy 31
cognitive therapy 29
   research outcome 38–9
common-factors approach 23–4, 27–8, 35, 42
   research outcome 37
complementarity 30–1
contact functions
   analysis of 167–71
contextual influences 66–7
Cooper, S. H. 91
co-regulation of affect 76
countertransference 68–9, 117, 118, 120–1, 129–30
   of psychotherapists 135–6, 152
countertransference dominance 70
creative adjustment 94–5, *96*, 99, 131, 135
culture 57
Cushman, P. 12

De Lise, G.   89, 95, 96, 97
Delworth, U.   134
Denzin, N. K.   12
Derrida, Jacques   13
Descartes, René   10
De Young, P.   80
diagnosis   89–90, 98–9
    classical psychoanalysis   90
    criteria   96–7
    Gestalt psychotherapy   90
    integrative approach   90–1,
        99–100
Diagnostic Statistical Manual (DSM)
    96–7
dialectical behaviour therapy   31
dialectical-intrapsychic process   70–1
dialogical-interpersonal process   70–1
dialogue   17, 19–20, 66
Doehrman, M. J.   133, 134
Dollard, J.   24
Downing, J. N.   8, 9, 14
dysfunctional behaviour   92–4
    analysis of   172–3

eclecticism   1
eclecticism, technical   26–7
ecological self   63
Ekstein, R.   134
Eleftheriadou, Z.   57, 58, 162
employment   159–60
Enever, A.   158
Epstein, M.   98
Erskine, R. G.   79
Espin, O.   58, 162
European Association for Integrative
    Psychotherapy (EAIP)   146,
    148, 156
European Association for
    Psychotherapy (EAP)   8,
    146, 159
Evans, K.   57, 91, 133, 134,
    146, 161
existentialism   21–2

family therapy   134
Ferenczi, S.   135
field theory   16, 97
Fishman, D. B.   39

five-relationship model   26
Fonaghy, P.   7, 24, 50, 51, 54, 55,
    56, 73, 76
Foster Report   157
Fourcade, Jean-Michel   146
Francis, A. J.   98
Frank, J. B.   8
Frank, J. D.   8, 24
Frankl, Victor   62
French, T. M.   23
Freud, Sigmund   9, 11, 23
Freud, Sophie   9
Friedman, M.   116

Gawalek, K.   58, 162
Gerson, S.   67
Gestalt dialogical psychotherapy   78
Gestalt psychotherapy   29, 66, 135
    diagnosis   90
Gilbert, M.   57, 133, 134, 146,
    148, 161
Glass, C. V.   36
Goldfried, M. R.   1, 8, 23, 29, 37,
    38, 40, 41, 42, 163
Gold, J. R.   25
Goodman, P.   110
Greenberg, L. S.   111
Guy, J. D.   130

Hargaden, H.   79
Hawkins, P.   134
Heath, G.   11
Hefferline, Perls   110
Holford, L.   13
holism   16, 59
Holland, L. A.   13
Holmes, J.   53
Horvath, A. O.   41
Howard, G.   59
Hubble, M. A.   41, 42, 43, 91
humanism   21, 24
Hycner, R.   66, 70, 71, 78, 79

I–It of relationship   17, 19–20,
    104–6
inclusion   53, 71–3, 131
'instillation of hope'   28
integration   1, 2

integration, theoretical 25–6
integrative movement 24–5
integrative psychotherapy
  conceptual framework 149–50
  core competencies 150–1
  cultural aspects 58–9
  diagnosis 90–1, 99–100
  different approaches to integration
    25–8
  epistemological base 15–17
  history 23–5
  philosophy 7
  process of 151–2
  purpose 151
  training 145, 146, 150
  training organizations
    (UK) 147–8
  values in clinical practice 18–20
interpersonal relationships 4, 53–7,
  95, 120
intersubjectivity theory 17, 65, 72,
  77–8, 99, 135
intrapsychic relationship 50–3, 120
introjection 93–5, 106, 113, 173
I–Thou relationship 4, 17,
  19–20, 103, 105–6, 115–16,
  122, 131, 162

Jacobs, Lynne 63, 70, 71, 79, 131
*Journal of Psychotherapy
  Integration* 145
*Journal of Transpersonal
  Psychology* 62
Jung, Carl 9

Karuso, T. 8–9, 58, 162, 165
Keisler, D. J. 99, 117, 120
King, Y. 59
Kohut, H. 33, 51, 55, 68, 77,
  104, 135
Krause, I. 57
Krueger, D. W. 50
Kuhn, T. S. 9, 60

Lachmann, F. M. 48, 76
Lambert, M. J. 41
Langs, R. 135
language of psychotherapy 29

Lapworth, P. 26
Lasch, C. 126
Lawson, H. 13
Lazarus, A. A. 27
Lewin, K. 134
liberal democracy 13
liberal humanism 11
Lincoln, Y. S. 12
Linehan, M. L. 31
Luborsky, L. 35–6, 38
Lyotard, Jean Francois 11

Mackewn, J. 53
Mahoney, M. J. 106
Mahrer, A. R. 149
Maroda, Karen 68, 69–70
Maslow, A. 62
Melnick, J. 90, 100
mentalization *see* reflective function
Messer, S. B. 29
Metzner, R. 60
Miller, N. E. 24
Mitchell, S. A. 79
Moustakas, C. 62
morality 18–19
mother–child relationship 32,
  48–50, 52, 125
  see also child development ;
    parent–child relationship

Naess, A. 60, 63
narcissism 33, 50, 52, 97–8
National Health Service
  (UK) 159–60
National Register of Psychotherapists
  (UK) 157
neuroscience
  as source of integration 32–3
Nevis, S. M. 90, 100
nihilism 14
Norcross, J. C. 1

object-relations theory 77
Ogden, T. H. 53, 67
one-person psychology 77
Opazo, R. 26
oppressive practice in psychotherapy
  161–2

Orange, D. 12
Orbach, Susie 48

Pannenberg, Wolfhart 64
paradigms 9–11
parallel process in supervision
133–4, 136–7
parent, adult and child ego states
55–6
parent–child relationship 127–9,
139–40
see also child development;
mother–child relationship
patient–therapist relationship
see client–analyst relationship
Paul, G. L. 35
Pavlov, I. 23
Pederson, B. P. 57
peer supervision 137–42
Perls, F. 14, 93, 99
personal development 19
process of 1
personality 22, 23, 95–6
phenomenology 15, 20
physical contact in therapy 124–5
analysis 170
Pilisuk, M. 60, 61
polarization 14
Polkinghorne, D. E. 13
Polster, E. 56, 93
Polster, M. 93
Poole, M. S. 134
postmodernism 10–12
*Power of the Countertransference,
The* 68
pragmatism 13
psychoanalysis 21, 22, 24
ironic and tragic vision 22–3
psychotherapists
competencies 152–3, 154–6
counter-transference 135–6
personality 23, 39
style of working 28–9
psychotherapist-supervisor
relationship 133, 134
psychotherapy
case study 83–6, 88–9, 91, 101–4,
106–8, 111–14

cultural aspects 57–8, 161–2
different approaches 33–4
education and training 9
intersubjective nature 73–5
nature of change 39–40, 41
relationship factors 40–1
schools 8
theories 11, 12
training 164–6
training organizations 162–3
psychotherapy research
studies 163–4
Dodo bird verdict 36, 40, 43
effects of allegiance and adherence
38–9
meta-analytic studies 35–7,
38
methodology 37–8, 42
on client 42–3
on contextual models 41, 43
on medical model 38, 40
'pure form' approach 1, 27, 29

Ramsay, C. T. 42
reason 10
Reason, P. 133
reflective function 7, 72
reflexive practice 133
relational psychotherapy 79–80
relational unconscious 67–8
repression 23
retroflection 112, 131
Ridley, C. R. 57, 59, 162
Rogers, C. R. 28, 68
Rosen, H. 11
Roth, A. 24
Rozak, T. 60
Rozenweig, S. 23, 35
Ryle, Anthony 31

Samuels, Andrew 57
Searles, H. 134
self-disclosure 116–17, 141–2
self-in-relationship 3, 47, 75, 78
domains of 3–4
self–object transferences 55, 104,
117, 121, 131, 136
self-reflexivity 51–2

self, the   20, 54–5
  relationship to body   47–50
  relationship to culture   57–9
  relationship to nature   59–61
  relationship to others   53–7, 77
  relationship to self   50–3, 120
  relationship to the
    transcendent   61–4
Shohet, R.   134
Sills, C.   79
skepticism, modern   10–11, 12–13
Smail, D.   162
Smith, M. L.   36
Society for the Exploration of
  Psychotherapy Integration
  (SEPI)   145
Sommer-Anderson, F.   48, 50, 54
Spotnitz, H.   130
statutory regulation
  United Kingdom   157–60
Stern, D. N.   48, 49–50, 61, 99
Stolorow, R. D.   53, 65, 67, 77, 78,
  79, 136
Stoltenberg, C. D.   134
Stricker, G.   25
supervision   133
supraparadigmatic model   26
surface behaviour   22
symptom substitution   22
systems theory   21

Tansey, M. J.   120, 121
therapeutic process   2–3
therapeutic relationship
  see client–analyst relationship

Thompson, J.   161
Tobin, S.   99
Tolman, C. W.   11
Tolpin, M.   55
transference   133, 135, 136
transpersonal psychology   62–3
Trautmann, R. L.   79
Trevarthen, C.   49
truth   10, 12–13
Turgenev, I.   64
Two chair work   108–10, 111

United Kingdom Association for
  Psychotherapy Integration
  (UKAPI)   148, 156
United Kingdom Council for
  Psychotherapy (UKCP)   8,
  146–7, 150, 157–8, 159, 163,
  164, 165

Varela, E. S.   58
'vicious cycle'   29

Wallerstein, R. S.   134
Wampold, B. E.   37, 38, 39, 41
Wheeler, G.   53
Wilber, K.   26, 62
Winnicott, D. W.   72, 77
Wolfe, B. E.   37, 38, 42, 163
Wright, K.   52, 53

Yalom, I. D.   28, 91
Yontef, Gary   71–2, 79, 91

Zinker, J.   107